BETTER
RICHER
FULLER

Published by FiSmart
5825 Feldspar Way
Birmingham, Al 35244
Copyright ©2017 by Fi-Smart, LLC

Cover design by Sheila Parr

Interior design by Alex Head (Draft Lab)

IBSN: 978-0-9985360-0-2

Printed in the United States of America

BETTER
RICHER
FULLER

How Building Your Financial House
Can Help Protect Your Loved Ones, Grow Your Assets,
and Free You to Live the American Dream

GREG POWELL

This book is dedicated to the love of my life, Peggy, who inspires me daily to live life to the fullest and who has believed in me throughout our marriage; to our three daughters, Sara, Audrey, and Lydia, who have always motivated me to be the best dad and man that I can be; and to my parents, Ray and Ann Powell, who challenged me to make the world a better place for all to live.

CONTENTS

Ackowledgments 1

Introduction 3

Chapter One: Laying the Foundation 9

Chapter Two: The Room of Dreams 27

Chapter Three: The Legacy Room 47

Chapter Four: The Lifestyle Room 61

Chapter Five: The Wealth Room 75

Chapter Six: The Financial Opportunity Profile Room 95

Chapter Seven: The Children's/Heirs' Room. 115

Chapter Eight: The Retirement Fulfillment Room 129

Chapter Nine: The Estate Planning Room 145

Chapter Ten: The Attic 167

Conclusion. 177

Powell's Laws. 183

Recommended Reading 185

About the Author 193

Index 195

ACKNOWLEDGMENTS

There are times in my life that the expression "thank you" just doesn't seem sufficient. Those individuals who helped me with this book deserve so much praise.

I want to thank so many people who have been there, helping me throughout this literary journey. My team at Fi-Plan Partners and our clients who have shared their life experiences have played a key role. Thank you so much!

I also want to say thank you to specific people who played a key role in making this book a reality. People like Lisa Beck at Fi-Plan Partners who was determined I would make the deadlines she had established to make this book successful. Your determination is inspiring! Chris Davis at Chris Davis Digital who convinced me to organize my thoughts into a transcript. Randy Archer whose video insight got me to open up and to put my thoughts on the page. Stephanie Land, who, as my writing partner, took my thoughts and put them into a written format as though my voice was coming off the pages. A big thank you to Sheila Parr for her creativity and book cover design; Lari Bishop and Alex Head of Draft Lab for their invaluable insight, design, and advice; Linda O'Doughda, whose editing was phenomenal; and David Ratner as my publicist whose persistent belief in me gave me the confidence to move forward and share this book with others. Additionally, I appreciate the guidance of Betsy Byrne and Shane Lea Murphy, from LPL Financial, who worked with the team to ensure regulatory compliance.

To my daughters, Sara, Audrey, and Lydia, who motivated me to walk my talk and to take time to enjoy this journey in life with them. And most of all, I want to thank my wife, Peggy, for her constant support and belief in me as I maneuvered through this literary maze. No matter how frustrated I became or how many obstacles I encountered, Peggy reminded me to stay focused on my dream. No one is successful by themselves. It is the relationships in your life that can be your greatest wealth.

Enjoy building Your Financial House!

INTRODUCTION

The American Dream means something a little different for everyone. To some, it's the chance to start a new life. For others, it's the opportunity to build something from the ground up. But I'm betting that few people know that when James Truslow Adams coined the term in 1931 in his book *The Epic of America*, he defined the American Dream as "that dream of a land in which life should be better and richer and fuller for everyone, with opportunity for each according to ability or achievement."[1] He elaborated on his concept thereafter, but it is those three words—Better. Richer. Fuller.—that I want to call to your attention.

You might expect that for me, as a financial planner, the anticipation of helping people get richer is what revs me up in the morning. It does, but it's not the only thing, not by a long shot. Because, the way I work towards helping people make their money grow is not just through savvy investments or access to a collection of sophisticated financial products, though I use both. It's through a process that is not only designed with the goal of creating and sustaining their wealth but also seeks to create and sustain their better, fuller lives. In other words, it's a process that helps people pursue their American Dream.

1. John Truslow Adams, *The Epic of America*, Greenwood Press, 1931, page 404.

What's my definition of a better, richer, fuller life? One that allows you to balance hard work with ample opportunities to pursue your passions and pet projects. One that gives you the means to enjoy yourself and make others happy.

One that allows you to donate time or money, or both, to institutions and causes that matter. One in which you are secure knowing that your loved ones are provided for no matter what. Above all, it's one that is free of anxiety and fear. I get to know a lot of people in my line of work, and very few meet me for the first time without expressing some level of these two emotions, even those who have achieved great success. Despite their different backgrounds and circumstances, these men and women ask questions that generally fall along similar lines: Will we ever have enough to retire comfortably? What will we do if our daughter doesn't get an academic scholarship? What will happen if my mother needs 24-hour care? In the worst cases, their apprehension has kept them from taking reasonable investment-related risk, with the result that they have never earned sufficient returns to give them the peace of mind they seek.

The best weapon against anxiety and fear is knowledge. Unfortunately, if there's one thing usually missing from the financial planning process, that's it—at least on the client's side. Most financial planners know what they're talking about, of course. Often, when clients hang up the phone or walk out of their financial consultant's office, they usually have only a vague idea of what was really accomplished, even if they like and trust their advisor. The paperwork and charts, the financial jargon, the discussion of global economics and volatility in the markets—it's just too much, even for some of the most educated, business-oriented individuals. After consulting with their financial planner, they might have a plan in place, but the clients may not be able to articulate what it is. And because they don't fully understand the plan, they continue to feel vulnerable. Their anxiety and fear don't go away. They stick around, lurking in their subconscious minds and occasionally surfacing to treat them to a sleepless night or two. What if? What if? What if?

That's why I created the Your Financial House process—to give people the knowledge they need to banish their anxiety and fear so they can get control over their finances, work to secure their future, and get on with the important business of enjoying their lives. Your Financial House (used interchangeably throughout the book with the abbreviation YFH) is a financial planning tool that allows you to draft a customized blueprint you can then use to pursue independent wealth as well as a lasting legacy. Clients have told me over and over again that the YFH process is not just unique; it's life changing. And because of that affirmation, I've written this book as my way of virtually taking people by the hand and walking them through the process.

There is something you should know before you read any further: While all of the information you'll find in each room of your financial house will help you focus your intentions and potentially increase your wealth, I will talk very little about your financial accounts. (In fact, you won't even look at them until chapter four). Many professionals in my industry just want to talk numbers, but I think talking numbers right off the bat is premature. In my experience, when people seeking financial advice see numbers, they tune out, not because they're unintelligent but because they don't understand how the numbers relate to them. A number only tells us half of our financial story. Asking and answering all of the questions posed in *Better, Richer, Fuller*, however, will allow you to see the whole story and thus identify exactly what that number might represent to you and your family, not just in terms of the stuff or the experiences the money can buy but in how it can help you achieve fulfillment.

After better than three decades in this business, I have found that individuals and families that ask and answer the big-picture questions and have a firm understanding of their goals, dreams, and values before drafting their financial plan consistently perform better than do those that approach financial planning simply as a means to material gains. In addition, once they reach their goals, they report high levels of fulfillment, which means they are enjoying their wealth, not just accumulating it.

By embracing such a holistic approach there are many goals that can be pursued, such as a young couple earning an average annual income has the ability to retire with more than a million dollars in their portfolio because they have a plan and strategy in place; a retiree launched a multimillion-dollar company that employs much of his extended family; a family fulfilled a lifelong dream of relocating to South Africa to pursue missionary work. These aren't just hypothetical examples; these are stories of real clients of mine who followed Your Financial House strategies and worked towards the lives they had always wanted. And now, with this book, you can too. *Better, Richer, Fuller* will empower you to:

- Identify your goals and dreams and create a strategy for pursuing them
- Seek to protect and grow your wealth
- Ask the right questions so you can make more effective decisions about your money and your life
- Enhance your lifestyle while decreasing your anxiety and fear
- Coordinate your financial strategies with your lifetime goals and estate plans

- Plan for the unexpected so that you stay on track, no matter what
- Engage confidently and communicate assertively with your financial advisor
- Follow through on the financial plan you create

Once you've walked through all of the rooms in your own financial house, you'll be ready to make the decisions and embark on the solutions that will bring your version of the great American Dream that much closer to fruition.

Better, Richer, Fuller is for anyone who is working hard and wants to grow what he has without sacrificing himself (and his relationships) to the rat race. It's also for anyone who has already achieved a high net worth and not only wants to protect her assets and secure her standard of living but also wants to make sure she passes her values on to the next generation. And it's a book for those to whom personal finance has always been a bit of a mystery, who have never been comfortable dealing with money, or who might have left the decision making to their spouse and now, following death or divorce, must take the reins. Financial planning isn't supposed to be overwhelming or confusing, and my hope is that after reading this book you'll even find it fun, surprising, and inspiring.

I'm not a life coach nor a counselor nor an educator, but in my role as a financial house builder, I often play all three roles. When new clients leave my office, I want them to feel knowledgeable and in control, able to say with a sigh of relief, "This is the first time I really understand what I have and how my money can work for me." And now, with this book in your hands, you don't have to be my client to feel that same way.

MAKE-READY

In real estate, a make-ready is a set of preparations done right before a property goes on the market. At the end of each chapter, you'll find suggestions for steps you can take or additional resources you can investigate to help you get even more out of the Your Financial House process.

Following the YFH system will also leave you with another hallmark of the American Dream—a house. Not one built with bricks and mortar, with shingles or white Carrara marble tiles, but one built of dreams, ambition, and even love—a safe, sturdy, well-constructed financial house that you will enjoy living in and that you will be happy to pass on. The principles offered in *Better, Richer, Fuller* have led thousands of people towards their American Dream and the better, richer, fuller life it represents. And you're about to become one of them.

Chapter One

LAYING THE FOUNDATION

"Will you color with me, Daddy?"

Surprisingly, that simple question is what inspired me to create Your Financial House.

It was a leisurely Sunday afternoon, and I was spending time with my youngest daughter, Lydia, who was sprawled out on the living room floor amid some sheets of paper and a box of crayons. It was an all-too-rare quiet moment. For the past seventeen years, I had worked in the Alabama branch of one of the country's well-known New York Stock Exchange firms. It was a busy life, and enjoying time like this with Lydia was not to be taken for granted.

"Sure thing, sweetheart. What should we color?" I replied, getting down onto the floor next to Lydia and pulling a piece of blank paper in front of me.

"I want you to draw me a house, please."

I'm no artist, but a house I could do. I plucked a black crayon out of Lydia's sixty-four-count box of Crayolas and drew a square. Then I topped it with a triangle and drew a horizontal line inside the square, creating a two-story structure. Lydia watched intently as I drew three vertical lines to designate eight rooms. At that, Lydia grabbed some of her brightest-colored crayons and started carefully coloring in a square. I picked up a crayon and leaned in to help with the coloring, but my daughter stopped me by putting her small hand over mine.

"Dad," she said firmly, "this room is for Boots." (Boots was our cat.) The tone in Lydia's voice told me that the color I had chosen—apricot—was not one Boots would approve of.

"And this one," she said, bending her head as she began to fill in another square with a vibrant shade of pink, "is for my American Girl dolls."

Grinning at my daughter's serious demeanor, I listened as Lydia continued to list the purpose for each room. One was for her two sisters to share. Another was for her stuffed animals. And suddenly, a thought hit me: my job as financial planner wasn't that different from the job of homebuilder. One professional works with stone and plaster, the other with stocks and bonds, but ultimately, both professions work to construct safe places for people to protect and grow their assets and prepare for the future.

What Lydia had asked me to do for her was quite similar to what my clients asked me to do for them, except that in the process of drawing her house, Lydia had given more thought to why she was building it than many people ever have or ever will. In addition, when her simple rendering was complete, she would be able at any time to look and see in black-and-white—or, rather, in aqua, fuchsia, and canary yellow—specifically for whom or what each room had been designated, and how each one connected to the next. Could there be anything more reassuring? Lydia's house was nothing less than a blueprint to security—her own and that of the people and pets and objects she loved.

I should draft a blueprint for my clients, I thought; one that outlines their needs and shows in exact detail how I can help them build their financial house to accommodate the people and pets and objects they love. But, I realized, I have no model for how to do that. Because, despite the countless soft-focused television ads put out every year by financial services companies (including my employer), each promising a personal touch and genuine concern for client welfare, generally we weren't trained to worry about our clients' needs and desires unless their single uppermost need and desire was to earn a better rate of return on their investments.

The more I thought about it, the more I knew I had to make a radical change in the way I communicated with my clients. No architect or general contractor would ever break ground on a new home without first having a long discussion with the owners about how they intended to use the house, who would live there, their preferences regarding the house's style and size, or what building materials, appliances, and finishing touches they envisioned. No one who decides to have a new home built would ever hand over a check to the architect without first reviewing a plan that showed how all of those details could be translated into a real house. I needed to have the same type of conversation with my clients so that I could better understand not just *what* they wanted, but *why*.

And then I'd go one step further. The bull markets of the 1980s and '90s had, in my opinion, made the investment industry lazy and too comfortable with its success; little was being done to improve service or upgrade strategies and advice. But once my clients' financial houses were built, I intended to come back for regular visits to make sure each house still suited its inhabitants. After all, sometimes we outgrow our homes and sometimes we need to downsize. It would be my job to make sure that my clients' financial houses were always perfectly customized for their lives.

With Lydia's permission, that very same Sunday afternoon I taped her colorful picture of a house to my home office wall, where it stayed to remind me of my epiphany. Thereafter, I started asking my clients more questions and documenting their feedback, which confirmed they were desperate to better understand their finances and to feel more in control of their futures. I also started noticing the inadequacies in my employer's software. At night I'd look at Lydia's picture and think about how people could change their lives if they learned to build a financial house. I believed in this house so much that when I left my company three years later, in 2005, I built my new business around it.

Since then, I've made it my mission to show people that the best way to acquire wealth isn't by working insane hours and obsessing over how to get the biggest returns. Your financial success rate has much more to do with your personality, your philosophy about money, and your ability to communicate honestly. Some individuals might be skeptical of a financial planner who cares as much about researching his clients' psychological profiles as their bank statements, but they wouldn't be if they could see how quickly after completing a Your Financial House (YFH) evaluation they start to feel that they are in control of their lives.

YFH'S SIX KEY DIFFERENCES

You might be asking how YFH could be significantly different from any other financial planning tool you've seen or heard about. Let's take a look at the six key ways this evaluation is different and more customized than other tools.

IT TEACHES YOU TO ASK THE RIGHT QUESTIONS

As you start building your own financial house, you'll be asked many, many, many questions. Now, that may not come as much of a surprise.

After all, you're looking for financial planning advice, so you're probably expecting to answer questions about your money. That's where many financial advisors start too. Ten seconds after meeting you they'll ask you when you want to retire. Then they'll want to know how much money you have, how much you want to earn, and how much risk you're willing to take to get it. In *Better, Richer, Fuller* I am going to ask you to think about money as well, but in a different way.

The conversations I will encourage you to have—not just with your advisor, but with yourself—will not revolve so much around how much money you have or want to earn, but what you want to accomplish with it, where you want it to go, and how you can best use it to reflect and even promote your values. Yes, I will ask you to think about your retirement, but I will also ask you to consider the relationships in your life that could affect it—and to make decisions accordingly. By the end of a conversation that helps them get to the heart of *why* instead of exclusively *how much*, people have a clearer vision of what strategies will work best for them and are more motivated to stick to their plans.

IT ESTABLISHES NEW GOALS AND REVITALIZES OLD ONES

When it comes to expressing what they really want, it's been my experience that most people lie—both to themselves and to their loved ones. To be fair, their lies are often ones of omission, not commission. As we get older, we often put aside our big ambitions or our hopelessly romantic dreams in favor of more practical, realistic goals; maybe we even forget we ever had those dreams. But forgetting doesn't mean they're really gone.

I sometimes use the analogy that, just as with a file you "delete" from your computer, your dreams from long ago are still inside your mind, they've simply been stored in a different place. And, as often happens, the questions and discussions during an YFH consultation help individuals retrieve their dreams from their brain's computer-like memory system. Within minutes, I will hear some variation on the comment, "You know, that was something I *really* wanted to do in life."

Sometimes I see clients' older dreams and passions come back to life, fresh and exciting, and they lead to new, exciting opportunities the client had never considered before. I've heard many of them say: "Wow, I never thought about looking at my life, my dreams that way. For the first time in a long time those hopes and dreams are no longer full of obstacles; they've become possibilities. And those possibilities give a whole new perspective on how I can live my life."

When we keep our hopes and dreams locked up inside our heads, it's impossible for us to realize how much they are affecting our important financial decisions. That's the beauty of this system. Your Financial House is set up to force honest conversations with all of the individuals who will be affected by your financial decisions, whether it's your loved ones, your financial planner, your business partner—or yourself. And once those dreams are out in the open, and you build your financial house, you'll usually find that they are neither as crazy nor as hard to achieve as you probably once thought.

IT'S PROACTIVE, NOT MERELY PREVENTATIVE

When it comes to financial planning, fear is often what finally gets people to consult a professional. Many advisors—even the ethical ones—take advantage of that fear, playing off that emotion and moving people to quickly commit to investments they really can't afford or really don't need. More discussion needs to occur. All advisors need to take more time to understand all of the issues and concerns within a person's life that can impact that person financially. That can't happen when you follow the steps in YFH because the process ensures that you have a solid understanding of the likelihood of your worst fears and what risks you can and cannot take to prevent them.

Here's a familiar example that illustrates how you should base your financial decisions on knowledge, not emotion. Let's say you're at a neighborhood social gathering and your friend starts talking about a hot low-priced stock he's just invested in. He brags with confidence about the many shares he's purchased, the many dollars he's committed. That night you continue to think about it, and the next morning you enthusiastically call your advisor to instruct her to purchase this speculative stock. After all, your friend put a lot of money into it; you want to do the same. Not once have you asked yourself if you can afford to lose that much money because your focus is on making so much money. It never occurs to you that this speculative stock could go under. How would that impact your future going forward? Is the risk really worth it, especially in light of you being on track to reach your goals anyway? Shouldn't you and your advisor analyze the company before you invest in it?

The YFH process enables you to separate the emotion from the facts, knowing that you don't need to compete or try to keep up with the "Joneses." You need to take on risk that can help you, not set you back. In addition, you'll be asked to use your imagination and consider scenarios that could alter your plans if they were to come to pass. The intent is not to scare you into making rash decisions but to encourage you to plan ahead for the unexpected.

There are no "what ifs" left when you build using the YFH process because it forces you to confront your fears and imagine all possibilities so you can incorporate contingency plans and safeguards into your financial planning portfolio. It eases your anxiety by giving you the knowledge you need to properly evaluate your risk and make an informed decision.

THE RESULTS ARE EASY TO UNDERSTAND AND VISUALIZE

Nothing hacks me off more than when someone tries to talk over my head with industry jargon. When my team and I talk to clients, we use language we know they're going to understand. The YFH process is designed so you can create your financial plan without once having to consult Investopedia. com. You will not have to decipher pie chart analyses or ponder the percentages of different market sectors in order to complete it. Instead, you'll think about your life and decide how you want to construct your future. By the time you have completed your own customized financial house, you should be able to have a meaningful conversation with any financial advisor in language you understand completely.

Another benefit is that by the time you're done, you'll have an easy-to-follow visual overview of everything that really matters to you. Consequently, when circumstances change—due to an unexpected birth or illness, a promotion or layoff, a marriage or divorce—you can quickly determine whether your financial house needs an add-on, a wholesale renovation, or a simple repair. Best of all, the system gives you and your money manager an easy way to discuss which financial tools will be most appropriate for the job.

IT TEACHES YOU TO MANAGE YOUR ASSETS AND INVESTMENTS THE WAY THE RICH DO

Extremely wealthy families—defined as those that can claim a net worth of at least fifty million dollars—often hire a private investment firm called a single-family office, or SFO. Devoted exclusively to their client, that company helps the family manage their trusts and portfolios as well as coordinate many other parts of their lives, from their real estate holdings to their philanthropic projects. YFH democratizes the SFO process, giving everyone access to that kind of personal attention.

Too many people don't realize how interconnected the different aspects of their lives are. For example, they will speak with their CPA about their taxes but not about their plan to liquidate an asset, when in fact, the CPA might alter her advice if she knew about the liquidation. Your Financial House breaks down those silos, ultimately bringing together *the financial advisor, the CPA, the estate attorney, the insurance agent*—all of the professionals in your life who can help you get to where you want to go. It will make sure you give them the information they need, make you aware of what questions they should be asking you, and help you coordinate your team.

IT'S A LIVING DOCUMENT

Even when life feels stable and steady, you'll take a yearly walk-through in your financial house so you can assess what steps you need to take to maintain and upgrade the value of it. Best of all, the process gives you and your money manager an easy way to discuss which financial tools will be most appropriate for the job.

I want to debunk the common myth that you have to *have money* in order to *make money*. I think it's dangerous. It encourages too many people to work too hard, or to think if they just get that pay raise or make that risky investment, they'll have it made. It's also an excuse people use to explain why they haven't financially succeeded the way they wanted to. I've met people with huge incomes who didn't have two nickels to rub together because they mismanaged their money, living as though tomorrow would always be like today. I've also met people who earned a modest income but set aside money from every paycheck and, as a result, were in an excellent position to steadily earn enough to satisfy not just their needs, but their wants too. And the funny thing is, if you met both types of people at a party, you'd probably guess that the people of more modest means were actually the wealthy ones from the way they held themselves. They are confident and optimistic, and they exude a sense of control.

I see this as evidence of a principle that I have long held to be true:

Powell's Law #1: Money doesn't give you confidence as quickly as confidence gives you money.

I believe the secret to wealth isn't to start out with lots of money, but to do something great with what you've got. And when you approach your finances with the well-earned confidence that comes from walking through the YFH process, you make the good decisions that help you focus on making what you've got a whole lot bigger.

THE GRAND TOUR

What have you got, exactly? And how are you going to know what to do with it? That's exactly what the Your Financial House process is going to help you ascertain. Though each person's financial house is custom-built, there is only one floor plan: it's a two-story structure with eight rooms and an attic.

your financial house™

the blueprint for financial growth & security

Self Actualization			
Esteem (Self-respect, autonomy, status)			
Social (Affection, belonging, acceptance)			
Security (Protection from physical and emotional harm)			
Physiological (Hunger, thirst, shelter)			

Financial Opportunity Profile Room	**Children's/ Heirs' Room**	**Retirement Fulfillment Room**	**Estate Planning Room**
Room of Dreams	**Legacy Room**	**Lifestyle Room**	**Wealth Room**

The cookie-cutter layout might irk your "inner" interior designer, but as you'll see, the purpose and location of each room has been carefully thought out, with each strategically positioned so that one feeds and adds value to the next. People ask me all the time why I aligned the rooms the way I did, and I suggest they take a moment to think about it. When they look at the first floor rooms they see areas of life that motivate most of us to work hard and strive for success. We want to be able to live our dreams. We want to live a life worth remembering, that made a difference in this world; we want our legacy to live on. We want a lifestyle that gives us the comfort, security, and other rewards we work so hard to achieve. And, finally, we want to accrue wealth. Dreams, legacy, lifestyle, and wealth are key to making a person's life fulfilling.

I also chose to align the four rooms this way because sometimes experts in the financial service industry overlook them. It's possible that a financial advisor will briefly discuss a person's goals in life and then immediately begin to describe investment products so that the appointment can end within an hour and the money can be invested. My hope is that you will see a huge quality difference as I walk you through each of the rooms in the YFH model.

We'll start in the Room of Dreams, because there's no point in talking about investments before establishing what it is you want to do with your money. Many people accumulate wealth but have no clear-cut goals for how to use it. Such an unfocused approach leads to a tremendous waste. We're going to get specific in this room, so instead of using the vague phrase "saving for retirement," you're going to say you want to retire when you're 68 and still be able to live in your current home, or instead of "travel," you would love to take the whole family on a cruise to Alaska. In this room you will also find out whether or not your dreams fit in with your career goals and they complement those of your partner, or anyone else whose life may affect yours. Once you've walked through the Room of Dreams, my hope is that you'll be in a much better position to use your money to bring those dreams to life.

Next we'll spend time in the Legacy Room, where we won't review what assets you want to leave behind when you die. Rather, we will discuss how you want to share your values—whether it's with your children or grandchildren, your city, your religious community, or a charity close to your heart—and extend your influence while you're alive.

Our next stop will be the Lifestyle Room. Don't worry; this is not where we put you on a budget…yet. It's where we will discuss how your lifestyle coordinates with your dreams and intended legacy. It's where you'll get a clear overview of how you like to live, how you save and spend money, and what gives you gratification. It's also where we'll determine whether you're ready to do what it takes to reach your dreams and goals, which could mean anything from cutting back at the office so you can do more volunteer work to buying a lake house where you can host whole-family gatherings. We'll explore how your lifestyle lines up with your goals. Are you really satisfied with your lifestyle? Does it bring you contentment, or does it increase your stress? Are you spending and saving in line with your lifestyle? You would be amazed at the number of people who say to me that the discussion we had in this room took a huge burden off their shoulders.

Next we'll enter the Wealth Room. We're going to look through your financial papers and assess your wealth, but we're going to do things a little differently from other assessment tools. The YFH process digs up assets that you probably never even thought to incorporate into your calculation of your net worth, like your health, for instance.

"My health?" you ask. Absolutely. This is another way in which the YFH process is different. Financial advisors always ask about monetary assets, yet that doesn't mean all of them help clients determine their net worth both in the present as well as in the future. They might overlook asking where the client wants to be net-worth-wise years down the road, and how they plan to take care of themselves to enjoy it. Sure, you can work hard and accumulate more wealth; but if it is at the expense of your health, you may wind up using those very assets to pay for costly health care should you become gravely ill or disabled.

Too often, I've seen clients whose monetary assets are scattered, their life, disability, and health insurance disorganized, and the person working so hard to stockpile wealth that he doesn't see the health ramifications coming his way. Since YFH is holistic, we look at the whole person and all aspects of his or her life and how money can impact them. We'll ensure that your wealth is not only accurately identified and organized but also actually working for you. We'll also get you set up so that you can make quick and easy adjustments when you're dealing with the vagaries of real life.

Our tour of the ground floor finished, we'll now head upstairs to the Financial Opportunity Profile Room. Here we'll figure out your tolerance for risk as well as calculate how much you really need to risk in order to fund all of the other rooms in your house and to achieve your goals and dreams. This means we'll analyze the risk in your portfolio in relation to the risks you might carry in your life, which can include everything from switching jobs or pursuing entrepreneurial opportunities to paying for your children's education or marrying someone whose attitude toward money differs from yours. The goal will be to balance your risks so you can reach your financial goals no matter what "Real Life" decides to throw at you.

Next door is the Children's/Heirs' Room. Whether you have kids or not doesn't matter in this room. Make sure you don't skip it. Everyone has relationships that can impact their money. It may be children, adult children, nieces, nephews, dependent parents, grandkids, and even pets. The point is, relationships of any kind can have an impact on your financial decisions, and your financial decisions can conceivably affect almost any relationship. Many people don't know whether their parents or in-laws may become financially dependent on them. A couple has a child with special needs, or another child develops a drug or alcohol addiction that adds extra expenses for rehab. A married daughter with three children goes through a divorce and moves back in with her parents, which results in financial stress. How do you plan to handle these unexpected circumstances? What questions do you need to ask and where can you find the answers? Time spent in this room will ensure that you've given enough thought to all of the relationships in your life while planning your financial house.

The tour continues with the Retirement Fulfillment Room, where we will plan how to make the most out of your post-employment golden years. In the Room of Dreams, you probably thought about retirement and what you'd like to do once you're no longer working. Here, in this room, we'll make sure that your dreams match up with reality. Many people are surprised to find themselves feeling lost once they leave the workforce, which can often lead them to make disastrous financial decisions as they try to stave off boredom or regain a sense of purpose. In this room, we'll encourage you to imagine alternate paths in case you decide the retirement you originally planned for isn't as fulfilling as you thought it would be.

The last room on the second floor is the Estate Planning Room. You'd be amazed at how much gets discovered here. People may find out that the paperwork they thought they had signed actually wasn't, or that they inadvertently negated the property terms outlined in their will after making a real estate transaction. No one likes to deal with this kind of paperwork, but in this room, we'll make sure you and your attorney have discussed two key areas: first, that you've reviewed all of the important documents that could be relevant in the event of your death or disability; and second, that your beneficiaries or executors will know what to do when the time comes.

The grand tour wouldn't be complete without taking a peek inside the Attic, of course, where we'll double-check our work to ensure that we haven't overlooked any assets. (You'd be surprised what people can forget—stock certificates in a desk drawer, saving bonds in a box in the closet, gold bars in a home safe, the list goes on and on.) In addition, we'll make sure you're comfortable with all of the decisions you've made up to this point so you can feel calm and confident as you go about your daily life. My goal is to have people tell me that it was the first time in their life that they could relax, knowing that all aspects of their financial life had been covered.

For many, home ownership is a sign they have arrived; a sign of adulthood, responsibility, perseverance, and growth; a symbol of hope for the future. A house symbolizes family and sanctuary. Building your own financial house helps you construct your financial strategy from the ground up, just as you would if you were building a real house. You will know that the foundation is solid, the walls are thick, and everything is up to code because you chose to design it that way. When you're done, you'll be able to move into this house confident that it is a warm, safe place where you will create all of the treasured moments and memories that transform a house into a home. Who would ever have thought a four-year-old daughter asking her dad to sit with her on the floor and color would develop into a moment that would transform and touch so many lives? As you continue to read this book, remember that you, too, have ideas, dreams, and goals that can improve your life and the lives of those around you.

Let's get started building your financial house. Start dreaming about what you want to do with your money and then turn the page to follow me into the Room of Dreams.

MAKE-READY

1. Get out a pen and notebook, your electronic device, or maybe, like Lydia, paper and crayons—whatever creative tools you prefer. Spend ten minutes drawing your own version of a financial house or go to our website at yourfinancialhouse. com and print off the YFH chart. As you read about each room, jot down whatever ideas, dreams, questions, or issues come to mind. Remember, this is *your* financial house. Your participation in furnishing this house determines the success and results you get from it. This should be an easy stream of consciousness exercise just to get your thoughts flowing.

2. Lydia planned her house to accommodate the people, activities, and possessions she valued most. Make a list of yours, especially those individuals who will be most affected by your blueprint.

3. Keep your note-taking tools close to hand. You'll need them as you continue to build your very own financial house.

Chapter Two

THE ROOM OF DREAMS

A few years ago I met a man I'll call Jerry. He had heard about me through a friend and had called to schedule a meeting to discuss his finances. On the appointed day, he showed up right on time, yet there was something slow and tired about the way he lowered himself into one of the comfortable chairs in my office. I had never met him before, but I know depression when I see it, and this man was hurting.

He explained that he had been forced to take his company's early out package. A man in his early fifties, he had expected to work his way up the corporate ladder and take his place at the executive level. This downsizing had thrown him completely for a loop. Gently, I asked him what he was afraid of. As he listed all of his concerns, he got increasingly agitated. What if he had already reached his professional peak? How was he going to make any money? What if he was forced to move his family out of state, away from friends and family, to follow a new job? How badly was this going to affect his retirement savings, especially since he had just lost a job with excellent retirement benefits?

Trying to bring the conversation around in a more positive direction, I then asked him to tell me about his strengths. He told me that he was a self-made man who had climbed the corporate ladder and maneuvered through the bureaucracy of his employer while earning a reputation for ethical behavior, honesty, and integrity. But within minutes he was ruminating again on how everything could fall apart with the loss of this job. "Greg," he finally said, "I am totally lost."

This was my chance. I looked Jerry in the eye and asked, "If you knew you could not fail, and money was no object, what would you do?"

Jerry hesitated. Then he said, "It's always been a dream of mine to start my own company." Pausing, he added, "But that's not possible."

Take two steps into my office and you can tell I'm an American history buff. A portrait of Teddy Roosevelt and several antique American flags hang on my wall, and my shelves are lined with American memorabilia and history books. Thinking fast, I pointed to a shadow box table in which I display my collection of presidential campaign buttons and mementos from both losers and winners.

"Jerry, look at these buttons. Some of these candidates had to run two or three times before they won. Abraham Lincoln lost more races than he won."

Jerry didn't react, but I rushed on excitedly, rattling off a list of people who had to lose big before they could win big.

"Babe Ruth led the major league in strikeouts. Michael Jordan got cut from his ninth-grade basketball team. Oprah Winfrey was fired from her first television news job. Walt Disney filed for bankruptcy and then announced to his wife that he was going to build a new company around an animated mouse named Mortimer. And you know, Jerry, my wife loves me, but she'd have me committed if I said something like that. Disney's wife, however, told him to name the mouse Mickey."

I went on, recalling how Lee Iacocca was fired from Ford Motor Company, which allowed him to revive Chrysler Corporation and become one of the greatest CEOs of all time, and that J. K. Rowling, then an unemployed single mom on welfare, was rejected by twelve different publishers before one finally agreed to publish her first Harry Potter novel.

"Don't give up, Jerry. You've got ideas and career knowledge that somebody is willing to pay for."

By now I was out of breath, looking at Jerry intently, hoping I had said *something* that would help him see that his career wasn't over. He just stared back at me with the same exhausted expression of defeat.

Finally, he stood up and shook my hand. "Greg, I appreciate your time," he said. Then Jerry walked out of the room.

THE BIG QUESTION

If you knew you could not fail, and money was no object, what would you do?

I asked Jerry this big question because I knew he would never think to ask it himself. Most people don't. It's a kind of pie-in-the-sky fantasy, something fun to think about but not to take seriously. But I believe that we should absolutely take it seriously, as seriously as we did back when we were little kids. Have you ever asked a child to tell you his or her dreams? You don't even have to preface the question with caveats about failure and money because those obstacles don't factor into children's thinking. It doesn't occur to them that there is any reason why they shouldn't discover a new planet, or make a time machine, or become a famous rock star. It's only when we become grown-ups that we start getting in our own way and setting limitations for ourselves.

When you set limitations, guess what you get? *Limitations.* But you can achieve anything if you take charge of your future and make a plan. And the first step in creating that plan is to recapture your childlike sense of possibility, answering this big question as thoroughly and as honestly as you can:

If you knew you could not fail, and money was no object, what would you do?

Write down your answer. And remember, you don't have to stop with just one. This is your chance to let loose your imagination and list as many possibilities as you want to.

Are you done? Congratulations! You just started building the first room of your financial house, the Room of Dreams.

I've heard some of the most marvelous and surprising answers to this question, often from some of my most buttoned-up clients. A conservative businessman admitted he always wanted to be a traveling bohemian artist; a woman informed her husband that she had secretly dreamed of going back to culinary school and opening up a restaurant, with some proceeds and food going to feed the homeless. I had to laugh at one client's incredulous expression when she turned in amazement upon hearing her husband share his dream: "You never told me you wanted a pickup truck!" But he did. A bright red pickup truck, in fact! He just never said anything about it because it didn't seem like a practical dream. As it turned out, he not only could afford it, his wife was more than happy to approve of the purchase.

Sad, isn't it, to think of all of the dreams that go to waste when people won't let themselves say them out loud, much less actually pursue them? Don't let that happen to you. Even if you're nowhere near achieving any of the dreams that show up on your list, don't think about them as things you'll do or have "someday." You may have your whole life ahead of you, but you're about to create a blueprint that will help you take steps toward achieving those goals. That's what Charles and Sarah, a young couple in their late twenties, did when they started building their financial house.

In their Room of Dreams, they determined that more than anything else in the world they wanted to pursue mission work in South Africa. Once we identified that goal, we were able to use it as our guiding star as we evaluated their assets and risks in every other room of their financial house. We calculated that to achieve their admirable goal, which would require relocating overseas, of course, they would need $1 million. Charles was an accountant and Sarah a fashion merchandise buyer; a million dollars was an astronomical sum for them. But they knew that reaching for the impossible dream held far more promise and potential for them than did steadfastly pursuing the reasonable, predictable, and utterly unfulfilling dreams for which they had settled. In three sessions over two weeks, we were able to draw a blueprint that could lead them in twenty years to the seven figures they needed. Keep in mind that Charles and Sarah were committed to achieving their goal and disciplined in their pursuit of it.

The blueprint included cutting expenses, selling the family car, and eating at home most of the time. Charles and Sarah were willing to do it all.

Charles and Sarah were no different from you. They had jobs, obligations, and family responsibilities they took extremely seriously and were sure would make moving to South Africa impossible. Had they stopped exploring their options after they came up with their answer to the big question, it's likely those commitments would have indeed kept them from achieving their dream. But they didn't stop there, because as soon as they started voicing all of the reasons why their dream was impossible to achieve, I informed them it certainly was not. All they had to do was *A.S.K.*

A.S.K.—the YFH Self-Assessment

What gets in the way of your dreams?

Anxiety.

Anxiety is a state of mind. It is worry with anticipation that something could happen in the future.

What helps people move forward to overcome their anxiety?

Strengths.

Each of us needs to understand that our strengths, talents, abilities, relationships, and assets will enable us to become successful. Strengths give each of us the ability to open up and see the possibilities.

What other sources can lighten your anxiety?

Knowledge.

By assessing your strengths and reflecting on what information you need to move forward, you will have sufficient knowledge to make sure you are making the right decision. A combination of strengths and knowledge will give you confidence to confront your anxieties.

HOW DO YOU ATTAIN KNOWLEDGE?

A.S.K. is one of the keys to making the Your Financial House process work for you. This short series of questions can lead you to identify your Anxieties, to assess your Strengths, and to gain the Knowledge you need to eradicate the fear that might be holding you back or increasing your vulnerability to making poor decisions that undermine your portfolio. A.S.K. is an important process of self-discovery whose results will stick with you long after you've left the Room of Dreams, influencing your decisions and guiding you through the remaining rooms of your house. As in the case of Charles and Sarah, "A.S.K.ing" is particularly useful when you discover a gap between you and your dreams. It allows you to bridge that gap and even to close it up. A.S.K.ing also puts you in a positive mindset so that when the unexpected occurs (and it will), you won't panic.

Here is where you need to get quiet and think about the topics of anxiety, strengths, and knowledge. I want to walk you through the process. You can print off the A.S.K. form from our website, yourfinancialhouse. com, or just take three pieces of paper and write one of the three words—Anxiety. Strengths. Knowledge.—at the top of each page. List all of the anxieties you have in your life. Itemize all of your strengths. As for knowledge, let your anxieties or worries help guide you to the information and resources (person, website, book, institution) you need in order to move forward. In essence, pose the question, "Who has the knowledge I need to motivate me to take action?" and list what areas you need to research or what people you need to contact.

Now let's look at each of these three steps in more detail so you can begin to move forward.

IDENTIFY YOUR ANXIETIES

You can't get rid of your anxieties until you own up to them, so the first step in the A.S.K. process is to write them down.

Go on, write them down. All of them.

I can almost guarantee that one of them will be about having enough money to last the rest of your life—that's the response I hear first and foremost from my clients. But there are surely others. Maybe you're worried that your job or industry is not as secure as it once was. Maybe your property taxes keep going up. Maybe you keep coughing and no one can figure out why. Maybe you have a child with special needs or dependent parents, or you suspect a family member is struggling with addiction. Maybe you don't know how you're going to pay for your child's college tuition.

Fear is a natural emotion. If you're crossing a street and you see a car speeding right at you, fear is what gets you out of the way. Fear is a very real and crucial response to danger, to a real or a perceived immediate threat. Anxiety, on the other hand, is the expectation of a future threat. Anxiety is real in that you feel it, yet it is far more subjective than fear is, and feeling anxious is usually an overreaction to a situation, the results of which can be uneasiness, nervousness, fatigue, and problems with concentration. Let me emphasize that I am not a medical expert; I do understand, however, that anxiety can come in all types and forms and people can allow it to control them to the point of it being crippling. It can cause suffering in the form of a disorder. The type of anxiety I see in so many of my prospective clients is the anxiety that results from a lack of knowledge and understanding. For purposes of this book, that is why I have stated that this type of anxiety isn't real; it's simply a state of mind. It's worry tinged with anticipation, and we bring it entirely on ourselves.

Anxiety occurs when we mentally paint ourselves into a corner and, seeing no way out, lose our hope and confidence. We feel anxious about what we can't predict or control because we don't believe that we'll have the wherewithal to solve a problem if it occurs. We can start, though, to work on nipping that anxiety in the bud by focusing on our strengths.

ASSESS YOUR STRENGTHS

You know that your anxieties weaken you, but do you know what makes you strong? Think about all of the ways in which you have succeeded in your life and list the strengths that got you there. Perhaps you were a stellar academic student. Maybe you're scrappy. Empathy, tenacity, and optimism are all strengths. So are good woodworking skills and a lovely singing voice. How about marrying someone who complements you perfectly? Almost anything can be a strength if it serves you well.

One of the nice consequences of completing this exercise is that it can help you discover strengths you didn't realize you had. Almost all of us are far wealthier than we realize, we're just usually measuring with the wrong stick. For example, a widow came to me to talk about her finances and I could see she was terrified. "My husband always handled such things," she said, fighting back tears. "Every time we met with the other advisor, I didn't understand all the charts and graphs, so I didn't ask questions. And now I don't know what I have or what to do."

I assured her she would soon understand her finances, but first I wanted her to A.S.K.

We started by assessing her anxieties. The list covered everything from her aversion to spiders to a fear of flying. Obviously, she was worried about having enough money to live on. She had never worked outside the home, so she felt doubly vulnerable now that her husband was gone. One of the reasons she didn't ask questions during her meetings with the other financial advisor was that she was afraid of looking foolish in front of others.

Next, we made a list of her strengths in light of her anxieties. When she found spiders in her home, she was kind enough to scoop them up and deposit them outside rather than kill them. Yes, she hated to fly, but she had nonetheless found enough gumption to take several trips around the world. She could still do the Lindy Hop and she read about two books per week. There were other strengths, too, of course, but the one she was surprised to recognize was her marriage. She had enjoyed a long, happy life with her husband, and he had cared enough about her to make sure she signed the legal documents that would revert all of their assets into her name should he die.

Knowing she would be well cared for in old age became an adjunct strength that eased her anxiety and made it easier for her to move on from her grief. And later, as we dug deeper into her finances and life insurance policies, we found that it was relatively simple to set things up so that her portfolio generated more than enough income for her to live on.

Focusing on your strengths also automatically diverts you from obsessing over your weaknesses, which is a complete waste of time (not to mention anxiety-inducing), unless you plan on turning them into strengths.

A great example of how a weakness can be turned into a strength pertains to my client Charles. The company he worked at was relocating to a different state, but Charles didn't want to move. He was considering starting his own business so he could remain in town. During our conversation he said: "I'm worried about making this big leap to start a business. I've never run a business before."

"Charles, you've been the head of your department for over fifteen years," I said. "You supervise the people. You interact with the clients. You create the budget and are accountable for it. Your new business will be just like the department you've been running all these years. The difference is you will own it. You're not giving yourself enough credit for your strengths!"

"I never thought of it that way," he replied. "I guess the pressure of having to make the decision just blinded me to what I was really doing."

"Exactly!" I agreed. "Play to your strengths."

Strengths such as stamina, creativity, and a rich professional network could lead to a lucrative second career. Strengths such as family, faith, and good health might allow you to take certain risks you might not have once dared to try. In the case of our widow, she eventually started using one of her strengths to help at-risk kids by volunteering at a literacy center.

SEEK KNOWLEDGE

As we just saw in the case of my widowed client, conducting a strengths appraisal leads to knowledge. And as we've already established, knowledge helps alleviate anxiety. In addition, a strengths assessment will often reveal where the gaps in your knowledge are causing your anxiety in the first place. Here's how it works.

Let's say you are anxious about losing your job. Your weakness is that your skills are a little outdated and you haven't interviewed in a long time. While there may be little you can do to control whether you get downsized or not, you can take steps to prepare for that possibility. For instance, you could (1) figure out how to network on LinkedIn; (2) ask a peer to review your resume; (3) find a career coach; and/or (4) take a relevant class at your local community college.

I'm constantly amazed at how many parents wait until their child turns sixteen years of age or older to consider college expenses. For those readers who have just had a baby or have a child or children under the age of ten, you need to research how much college tuition and room and board costs and work that into your budget as soon as possible. Learning to set aside money each month now toward those expenses is far better than scrambling a year or two before your child starts college. Also, don't always count on your child receiving an academic or an athletic scholarship. In the YFH process, we plan for the worst and strive for the best. That takes a lot of stress out of your life. Besides, it's always better to know what you're dealing with rather than to be pestered by a little voice in your head threatening that you're going to go broke trying to send your child to college. Do your best to set such a payment system up with the help of your financial planner and hold yourself accountable to implementing your plan. Knowledge gives you confidence.

Now that that's done, start looking around for other college aid options. There are many more scholarship opportunities out there than most people realize. If your children are old enough, talk to them about your concerns and, together, explore ways in which they might be able to start contributing to their own college fund. Every answer you come up with should push your anxieties further and further away. Information is power.

Our health is another issue that we get anxious about from time to time. What if a nagging cough turns out to be cancer? Anyone would be scared by such a diagnosis. But your anxiety and fear can spur you to action, not apathy. Be strong and ask yourself, "Do I have the best doctors working on my case? Is there a better treatment option, or a better doctor, located out of state? Who do I know who can help me with these decisions?" In other words, have you done everything you can, and acquired all of the knowledge you need, to give yourself the best odds? If not, now is the time to start.

A.S.K.ing in any situation leads us to the solutions we need or, at the very least, gives us the satisfaction of knowing that we have done everything in our power to make a bad or undesirable situation bearable, and maybe even acceptable. It won't guarantee, unfortunately, that you will see the outcome you desire, but it can make the time you do have infinitely more productive and positive for both yourself and your loved ones. And that's worth a lot.

Seeking knowledge not only eases your anxiety, it also maximizes your strengths. And when that happens, your life gets better and more opportunities to live your dreams will come your way.

AN ONGOING PROCESS

One day a man who had already gone through the A.S.K. process called to tell me he needed to get "more aggressive" with his investments. I wasn't so sure. He had already designed his YFH blueprint, and a quick glance at his portfolio revealed that it was performing right on target. The kind of aggressive investments he was proposing could jeopardize everything he had already built.

Rather than automatically do as he instructed, I asked, "Why do you want to change the plan?"

I learned that he was going through a divorce, and on top of that, his adult child suddenly needed money. His problem was not his portfolio's return but the anxiety he was suffering as a result of these two crises. I urged him to work through the A.S.K. process with me once more before he made any decisions.

Keep in mind this is an excellent example of how the A.S.K. process is ongoing. I personally reevaluate my A.S.K. diagram every month, whether I think I need to or not. I want the A.S.K. process to be a habit in my life. And that's what I wanted my client to grasp. As his life circumstances changed, so did his finances. So, even though he and I had gone through the steps of A.S.K. before, we needed to do it again to eliminate any new anxieties that had arisen, to utilize all of his strengths, and to make sure we had evaluated all of the avenues of knowledge that would give us confidence: confidence that he would make a wise decision and confidence that I fully understood the circumstances and how they could impact him financially.

He agreed, and right then and there we started to identify his anxieties. You can probably guess what those were.

Then we assessed his strengths. He had always been confident, determined, and goal-oriented. Yet now he realized that in the time since he had conducted his last A.S.K. YFH Self-Assessment, he had lost focus. He was spending his time ruminating on his problems instead of concentrating on solving them. For example, he had once been the top salesperson in his corporation, but his personal problems had become so burdensome, he was not as productive. If he focused on his strengths and what he could control, however, such as meeting his sales goals, he would be in a better financial position to help his daughter. In addition, he needed to help her understand that while he was always there for her, she had a responsibility to solve her own problems. With his broad base of business contacts, he could help her network and open a few doors as she pursued finding a job that would support her and her kids.

Like many people do in the face of a dilemma, this man's initial impulse was to throw money at the problem; but in the end, the A.S.K. process allowed him to figure out that the solution lay in changing his attitude and readjusting his relationships instead of putting his financial security and future at risk.

You might be asking yourself this question right about now: "If the A.S.K. process is as effective for easing anxiety as Greg Powell says it is, why did someone who had already gone through that self-assessment once go into such a panic when things started going all wrong in his life?"

And my answer is this: although the A.S.K. process is indeed effective, it is not a permanent solution. You're only human, after all. Every day something will change, and change can make things better for you or awful. If it's the latter, you're going to react, emotionally. But it's always helpful if you know that when you feel anxiety, you can just go through the same process you went through to get rid of it the last time it hit you. A.S.K.ing gives you a way to initiate a dialogue, either with yourself or with your financial advisor or the other professionals who are helping you manage your personal assets, so everyone understands the reasoning behind your decisions.

Besides, it's always good to check in with yourself, take stock, look around, and see where you might need to give yourself a little attention. Let's face it. Anxiety can cause you physical pain. It can age you. It can cause fatigue and frustration. You probably have heard people who built a real home from scratch tell how it caused stress in their lives. The same applies to Your Financial House if you don't embrace the need for upkeep, renovation, and cleanup in each room. To keep the value of your net worth up—or, in this case, the value of that financial house appreciating—you need to periodically review the topics in the YFH process so your financial house doesn't get sloppy or out of control. As the owner, you need to take care of yourself and Your Financial House. You can't move into a house with a nice yard and then never weed, fertilize, or mow the lawn. There will be times when a storm blows through that breaks a window or makes the power go off (sometimes that storm will be caused by you). But when it does, if you're ready to A.S.K., you'll find that even if you don't have the know-how right away, you'll be confident that you will be able to get the information you need to fix the damage and make the house secure again.

There's no need to fear storms when you know how to A.S.K. Besides, sometimes it's the storm itself that inspires your newest dream.

Powell's Law #2: There is no magic formula. Only your attitude, beliefs, and knowledge can move you forward.

DREAM BIG

Remember Jerry from the beginning of the chapter? His story isn't over. I thought about him a lot after he left my office, wondering how he was managing. I suspected I'd never hear from him again, but I was wrong. A few days after our first encounter, my phone rang. It wasn't Jerry, however; it was his wife, Cheryl.

"Greg, I'm calling to tell you two things. First, Jerry is headed over to your office now to bring you some financial paperwork he needs your help with. Second, I want to thank you. I have no idea what you told him, but he is a different person than when he came to see you. When he came back from your office, he was smiling for the first time in weeks. He's suddenly all fired up. He wants to start his own company!"

That was years ago. Today the "not possible" business Jerry built is booming. Jerry and Cheryl's children work for the firm.

What caused Jerry's remarkable about-face? As he told me in our second meeting, all the way home he kept thinking about our conversation. He had spent the few weeks prior to contacting me surrounded by his colleagues who were also reeling from being laid off; not one of them had suggested that the turn of events could actually be an opportunity. And yet, remembering the list of anxieties he'd given me, Jerry realized that if he quit worrying and started working toward solutions to the obstacles he envisioned, those obstacles—and with them, his anxieties—would disappear. And if they disappeared, he was left with no reason to think that his business plan wouldn't work. By giving himself permission to look beyond his anxieties, he remembered his strengths and he found empowerment. By the time he walked through the back door of his house that evening, starting his own business didn't seem like such a crazy idea anymore. In fact, it was starting to seem crazy that he hadn't done it sooner! All he had needed was a little more knowledge.

Knowledge is what keeps our dreams from becoming nightmares. If someone tells me their dream is to convert their family home into a special events venue, I'm going to ask what they know about that industry. I will help them gather the information they need to evaluate their strengths and reveal the risks they will be up against. Not everyone's dreams match their reality. For example, one couple who came to me insisted that one day they'd fulfill their dream of owning a farm. To me, the natural question was, what do you know about farms? Well, as it turned out, nothing. So then I asked them why they thought they'd like to own a farm. The answer? Less stress. Recalling what I had heard about the backbreaking work of running a farm, I suggested that maybe we should all do some research into animal husbandry and crop maintenance. In the end, the couple came to the conclusion they weren't going to pursue that particular dream. But through their research and conversations, they discovered that the dream had never really been about running a farm; what they truly wanted was to spend lots of time outdoors and to have a more relaxed lifestyle away from the stresses of the city. Their happy ending? They bought some horses and a place in the country.

This was the same kind of conversation Jerry needed to have with his wife, his family, and me after he decided to pursue his dream. We conducted a more in-depth A.S.K. process to confirm that he was prepared for everything that launching one's own business entailed. Over the course of a few weeks, a blueprint to a financial house was designed with the goal of keeping a steady roof over his family's head while Jerry embarked on this new adventure.

People often stick to safe dreams, but I do hope you'll also let your imagination go. Give yourself permission to get beyond your anxiety and fear to ask for things you don't think you deserve. You might be surprised at what you can make happen. Remember the man who shocked his wife by admitting he'd always wanted a red truck? He didn't consider it a practical dream because he was sure he couldn't afford it. We discovered by A.S.K.ing that he was scared to tell his wife he wanted to spend that kind of money on a car. But now he knew from his wife's reaction to learning of his dream that she would support that purchase. And I knew that he could, in fact, afford it. So while I took the couple to lunch, one of the other guys in our office called around to local truck dealerships, and we arranged for the couple to visit five different dealerships. That afternoon, the man bought a new red truck and drove it to our office, honking the horn with excitement as he pulled in to park.

Imagine what could be accomplished, and what problems could be solved, if everyone regularly committed to A.S.K. Here's a recent example to show you what I mean.

I was eating alone at a Ft. Worth restaurant. My waiter wasn't busy and we struck up a conversation. He explained he was a frustrated actor, waiting on tables between roles. I suggested he devise a more flexible game plan that allowed him to work his schedule around auditions.

"How am I supposed to do that?" he asked.

I asked if he had an iPhone and iPad. He confirmed he did. I then suggested he start a business interviewing small business owners, using his skills to produce videos for local websites. "It's evident you know how to ask questions," I said. "And you know how to be in front of a camera. So you can turn those skills into a business, coaching business owners on how to promote their firms by talking about their products online."

He then asked me where I came from. I told him Birmingham, Alabama.

"No. I mean, the past four weeks I've been struggling with how to have balance in my life, working long hours at the restaurant and not being able to prepare for auditions. You show up out of nowhere and here you are, answering that question for me. I can absolutely do what you're suggesting. It really is perfect for me."

That young man may or may not have a career in acting, but I'm certain he will become an entrepreneur. It gives me a great sense of satisfaction to think I might have helped him figure some things out using my strengths (organizational thinking) and knowledge (experience as a business owner). But more important, I was able to help lead this young man to recognize his own strengths, ones he didn't even realize were adaptable for anything other than the stage and screen. If he continues to A.S.K., he will surely find other ways to capitalize on his strengths, minimize or shore up his weaknesses, and build a bright future.

Take control of your life. Give yourself permission to dream big, to leave behind your anxieties, and to ask for the moon. If you want it badly enough you can make almost anything happen. And once you've gone through this process, you'll not only have a dream to hold on to, you'll be far better prepared to make the good investments and smart decisions to make it a reality.

It is at this point, as their dreams become a reality, that people tell me they want to share those dreams with others. Dreams becoming a reality really aren't that fulfilling unless others experience them with you. Make sure you complete the questions in the Make-Ready section of this chapter as preparation for being ready to walk into the Legacy Room. For that's where you can express your desire to share your dreams, help others achieve their dreams with your support, and create a legacy or memory of you that will last forever.

MAKE-READY

1. Retrieve those creative tools you used in chapter one, "Laying the Foundation." Begin listing what came to mind as you read about what might be included in your Room of Dreams. Ask yourself this chapter's opening question: "If I knew I could not fail, and money was no object, what would I do?"

2. Jot down in another list some dreams you may have pushed aside as "not possible." Reevaluate those assumptions, and start researching what it would actually take to make them possible.

3. Walk through the A.S.K. process. Note your anxieties, assess your strengths, and evaluate what knowledge you need to reach your goals or break down the barriers that seem to limit access to the goals you itemized.

4. Don't forget to ask your spouse or children about their goals. Start a dream dialogue with those closest to you.

Chapter Three
THE LEGACY ROOM

You just learned how the Room of Dreams helps you establish a vision for your life and all of the things you want to accomplish while you are still on this earth. The Legacy Room helps you establish how you want to be remembered after you leave it. This might strike some people as premature. "Only two rooms into planning our financial house and already you're asking us to think about the assets we're going to leave behind when we die?"

That depends on how you define assets. Our legacies are shaped far less by the money and far more by the values and ideas that we pass on. Think about it. When you read that a millionaire left a fortune to a library or the Cystic Fibrosis Foundation, after a few days you probably forget the exact amount the benefactor bequeathed. Am I right? What you do remember, however, is that the millionaire must have really loved books, or must have had personal experience with cystic fibrosis to bestow such a generous gift to that institution. The gift tells you something about who the individual was and what mattered to him; and by calling your attention to this library or that foundation, he has just spread his influence a little bit wider than he might have otherwise.

The truth is, most of the super-wealthy start thinking about their legacy long before they are gone simply because it's a good tax strategy. The rest of us usually don't have enough to warrant thinking about it quite so far in advance. But we should, whether we think we'll have a million dollars at the end of our lives or a few thousand. Because if we don't, whatever dreams we actually do accomplish in our lifetimes will ultimately be hollow. Fulfillment is the key to enjoying all of those goals and wishes we listed as we stood in the Room of Dreams, and we find fulfillment when we feel confident that we are making a difference and having an impact—even if it's just in our own small way—on the world.

Powell's Law #3: No one can enjoy success or fulfillment without touching the lives of others.

The Legacy Room encourages you to think about the causes, charities, and especially the people that you want to see participate in your success while you're alive, and on what terms.

I'm living proof of how the values people share during their lifetimes can continue to spread long after they're gone. The son of a steelworker, my father, whose hard work earned him a successful career originally as an accountant and then later as a financial advisor, had a favorite saying: "You're only as big as the world you create." To that end, I was taught that one of my goals should be to always seek out opportunities to learn, to reach out to others, and to share what I had. Money was nothing more than a tool for doing good. For example, it was simply assumed that if I wanted a soft drink, and my friend who was with me couldn't afford one, I would buy one for each of us. Those lessons and expectations influenced my decision to study finance. Not only did I want to learn how to make money from the markets, I also wanted to show others how to make money. I guess I figured that if more people knew how to invest, more people could buy someone else a soft drink.

Now I'm trying to pass those values to my children as I encourage them to pursue their dreams. My daughters might consider this spirit of generosity my legacy, but in reality, I'm just continuing my father's. And therein lies the beauty: his values live on and continue to do good in the world even when he's no longer here to do it himself. For a legacy to truly take hold, we need to explain it to the people with whom we want to entrust it, and we can give it even longer reach when we include them in its creation. (Incidentally, that's why the Children's/Heirs' Room is located directly above the Legacy Room in the Your Financial House design. Because most often it is your children and heirs—as well as your friends and your community—whom you want to experience a memorable life with as well as bequeath your legacy to so your values live on forever.)

It doesn't matter if you don't have much now. If you build a strong financial house, one day you will; and when that time comes, your Legacy Room will already be furnished and you'll know exactly what to do. I'm a firm believer that if you can see your success in your mind, you can make it happen.

Should all of this talk about fulfillment and legacy sound a little hokey to you, or if you're the type who needs to know there's a true return on investment (ROI) here, I can give you a solid, practical reason why you should take this chapter seriously. Namely, when we think ahead about how to bequeath our values and not just our material assets, we can significantly improve our chances of avoiding the "shirtsleeves to shirtsleeves" phenomenon, in which wealth built up by one generation is grown by the next, then spent and depleted by the third. You built your wealth through a certain combination of strengths and skills that no one else will be able to replicate exactly. Yet it will be able to survive and continue to grow if you take the time to have the right dialogue, not only with its future caretakers but also with the professionals who will help you execute your legacy properly.

Too often, people don't know where to begin a dialogue with others to assure themselves that they are making a difference in the lives that matter to them. That's where the YFH process is so beneficial. It helps you define who you really are in terms of your values and beliefs. And the issues you'll consider in the Legacy Room give you the opportunity to start those critical conversations right away.

WHAT DO YOU STAND FOR?

Basically, there are two types of people: those who already know exactly what they stand for, and those who aren't quite sure yet. If you'd place yourself in the latter camp at this point, you won't be by the time you finish reading this chapter.

Regardless of which type of person they are, everyone starts to identify what they stand for by answering the same question:

How do others perceive me?

Spend some time thinking about what you hope comes to mind when others think of you. Now, it's possible there's a difference between how you think people perceive you and what they really believe. The only way to find out, of course, is to ask. Make a list of the ten people whose opinions matter the most to you. Your list will probably include friends or family, but you could also include coworkers, clergy, or teachers. Then set up a time to talk to each of them. Explain what you're trying to do, and ask them for their honest impressions of who you are and what your actions say about you. If you wanted to get really honest feedback, you could even send out questions via the free package on SurveyMonkey.com, or some other online survey tool, so that their answers remain anonymous. Questions like these have elicited valuable feedback for my clients:

- What stories would you tell about me to explain what kind of person I am?
- What do my actions say about my attitude toward life?
- Has there ever been a time when my words and actions weren't aligned?
- Do my words and behavior match the values and beliefs I've told you I hold dear, or does there seem to be a little disconnect?

Make sure that you give your respondents plenty of leeway to offer criticism, and try not to get defensive about it.

The point here is not to open yourself up to a total personality make-over. Rather, the information you gather at this stage is purely for your own enlightenment, and it gives you a starting point. If you've got a firm set of convictions and everyone around you confirms that you're living them on a daily basis, that's good to know and it should help you feel confident as you move further into the Legacy Room. And if you're not really sure what values are most important to you, the feedback you get may paint the picture quite plainly. Sometimes it's hard for us to give ourselves a fair evaluation. Though some individuals may go a little too easy on themselves, most people conducting this exercise are probably too self-critical; we tend to see other people much more clearly than we do ourselves.

For instance, one client who was a grandmother explained how she saw her legacy taking shape through her grandchildren's desire to know more about her past and why she believed in helping others. She reminded them that she had lived through the Depression, and even though her family was not impacted, her father made sure the family helped other families in need. "One of my grandsons pointed out that maybe that explained why I didn't give to organized charities, because I wanted to make sure the families in need received the help directly," she told me. "This conversation brought me closer to my grandkids and I now know what is important to them as well. I also see myself playing a greater role in their lives."

When you've completed each interview or have reviewed the results of your online survey, you'll have a much deeper understanding of the type of person you are and what you want to be known for. Then you'll be ready to ask each respondent one last question:

How can I help you?

With that question, you are guaranteed to start furnishing your Legacy Room. Because, really, helping others is what building legacy is all about. If you've already started, great! And if you haven't, now you know where to begin.

Sometimes people who have already achieved some financial success are reluctant to ask this question because they're afraid the answer will be a request for money. In this case, you might use the information you gather, as well as the answers you came up with during your own A.S.K. self-assessment in the Room of Dreams, to create a comprehensive list of your strengths. Remember, your strengths can include anything, including your perspective, skills, experience, contacts, relationships, wealth, and personality traits. Use this list to guide you toward figuring out the knowledge you need to determine where these strengths would be wisely invested, and whom you should ask the "How can I help you?" question. You can do this, too, if you're interested in branching out beyond your close inner circle and extending your influence into the wider community. Doing good can be addictive!

Let me give you an example of how all of the YFH rooms are interconnected to the question "How can I help you?" And, since we've been in the Room of Dreams and are now in the Legacy Room, let's look in particular at how these two rooms work together.

My client Ben had a very successful career in the steel industry, and the YFH blueprint we created showed him retiring at age sixty-five. At age fifty-one, however, he was offered an excellent early-out package, which would totally change his YFH blueprint. Financially he was sound, but he and his wife, Kathy, still had two teenage children to put through college and Ben was too young to retire.

At the start of our meeting, I asked Ben the same question I shared with you in the Room of Dreams: "If you knew you couldn't fail and money were no object, what would you do with your life?" His answer might surprise you—just as it did me. "I would love to be an athletic director at a university."

"Then let's see how we can make that happen," I said. But Ben was incredulous. "There's no way that can happen due to my lack of experience, but I would love to have that second career and inspire the lives of student athletes." At that moment I heard the making of a dream into a reality and a statement that sounded like a legacy goal to me. I wrapped up our conversation by asking Ben to make a list of all of the people he knew who had connections to universities, athletics, academics, and fundraising. I asked him to treat this as a journey, not as a panic attack, because he had to find a job within a week.

Ben returned a few days later with his list of anyone and everyone he could think of who might have a connection. We discussed the list and I suggested that he should contact all of them, asking if he could have thirty minutes of their time to share his dream and his legacy goals. "Most importantly, Ben, ask them if they can make additional introductions for you. Emphasize the strengths that you will bring with you from the steel industry. At the end, after they have answered how they can help you, ask them how you can help them. Open up your contacts. Let them know you are sincere. Then make sure you live up to your promise—help them. It will all come back to you tenfold."

I am proud to tell you that Ben is currently an associate athletic director at a university. Because he never gave up, emphasized his strengths, and had so many contacts who gave him further references, the doors opened for him. He fulfilled his promise of helping the university by showing that his astute business background enabled him to raise money for university athletics faster than someone who had been only in the academic arena. Ben's dream came to life and his legacy of having an impact in many student-athletes' lives is well on its way. And his children were impressed with what their dad achieved as well as the confidence he had during this time of transition. Ben's legacy in his family is alive and well.

KEEP THE CONVERSATION GOING

Having completed the exercise above, you can now clearly articulate your Legacy Room values, and you want to make sure your immediate heirs learn to live by them as well so they can act as good stewards of your wealth. It's going to take a little training. You can and should certainly model the kind of behavior and approach to life you want to instill in others, but when it comes to teaching people how to handle money wisely, it's better to be explicit than to assume everyone will know what to do when you're no longer around to guide them.

One popular way to ingrain a sense of fiscal responsibility in younger generations is to create a new family tradition centered on building legacy. Often families schedule this during the holidays at the end of the year, yet other families make it the centerpiece of a family vacation. The grandparents might put the money in for charitable contributions, but it could be the parents as well. Some families give charitable allowances so the kids themselves decide where the money goes. The main point is that the family talks about their values and beliefs and then takes action to show that those values and beliefs are part of their legacy. Freedom needs to be given in the dialogue so that the younger generations have input and a thorough understanding that helping others is a key part of the legacy of the family. Regardless, over the course of the year they put aside a certain amount of money. During the annual family meeting, the heirs gather to decide what to do with that money. It could be $5,000 on the table, or much more or much less. The dollar amount is less important than the process is. Each family member is encouraged to contribute to the conversation, perhaps sharing a list of the causes to which they want to contribute, whether it's a worthy charity or a tuition-poor college student. The family then decides together how to disburse the money, in full or in part. In the process, you'll each be communicating your core values related to work, faith, charity, and character.

Over the years, each family member will become increasingly attuned to others' needs, but in addition, they will learn how to evaluate when money can—and cannot—be used to meet them. In this way, you will be able to have a part in teaching your heirs how to be good stewards of the money you have made. In addition, by making legacy-building a participatory event, you get to help create incredible memories while imparting your value system and getting the chance to explain how and why it has been intrinsic to your success.

Whatever you do, don't get fixated on the idea that your heirs will have to hold exactly the same beliefs that you do, or focus their efforts in precisely the same way you have, in order to honor your legacy. For example, in walking clients Amy and Tom through the Legacy Room, they seemed visibly uncomfortable when I asked them whether they had taken steps to share their values with their daughter, Sheila. Tom reluctantly admitted that they weren't sure Sheila believed in any of the values they were trying to teach her. She had started dating a boy they didn't think was a good influence, and her dress and attitudes of late had changed dramatically.

As I've said before, I'm no counselor. But I've sat across from enough parents to know what questions might be helpful at this juncture.

"How do you interact with your daughter?" I asked.

Amy and Tom began to list the ways they spent time with Sheila. They insisted she eat dinner with them every night; they attended her activities at school; they took her on trips. Clearly they were involved, supportive parents. Still, Sheila seemed distant and sullen, more focused on the boyfriend than on her family.

I knew from our earlier discussion in the Legacy Room that Amy and Tom were active in several charities. I asked them whether they had ever discussed their involvement with those organizations with Sheila. They said she had limited interest in those efforts. So I suggested they sit down with their daughter and tell her they'd like her to pick a charity the whole family could get involved with. Then I suggested they not only make a significant financial contribution to that cause but also offer Sheila funds with which she could make her own donation too. Most important, I encouraged them to volunteer together for her cause.

My clients agreed to try. A few months later they were back in my office. The couple who had left my office with tears in their eyes seemed to have undergone a transformation. Their smiles lit up the room.

"Everything is different at home," Amy said. "When we asked Sheila which charity she wanted to help, she chose a homeless shelter. So we gave her some money so she could make a donation in her own name.

"Then the three of us started serving meals at the shelter once a week. We really enjoyed working together. And when she saw the needs there, Sheila initiated a coat donation drive at her school to benefit the shelter.

"Next thing we knew, she broke up with her boyfriend. When I asked her why, she said, 'He's so demanding of my time. And I've got more important things to do.'"

Sheila may not have valued specific causes as much as her parents did, but by sharing the contents of their Legacy Room with their child, Amy and Tom allowed her to start carrying their values into her own unique room. They are now confident that their daughter will honor, respect, and do her best to uphold their legacy whenever the time comes for her to take the reins herself. They also discovered one more benefit to spending time in this room—the process can actually deepen and strengthen your relationships.

SHARE WHAT YOU KNOW AND LOVE

Even if you don't have children or direct heirs, you can still ensure that your legacy will live on and perpetuate the values you embrace. The key is to identify your passions. Once you know what they are, you can start researching which organizations will be the most likely to continue the legacy you're building now. I once had a client who had no immediate family, but adored her pets as though they were her own children. She also volunteered at the local animal shelter. It made complete sense to allocate a significant part of her assets to that shelter. And since she made the decision long before there was any pressing reason to, she was able to talk to the leaders of the organization and ask them what kind of help they most needed, then make the necessary arrangements on her end. The whole process gave her peace of mind as well as a great deal of pleasure.

And you don't have to make a grandiose gesture, either, to guarantee that your legacy takes hold. Camp Smile-A-Mile in Alabama is an example of a fantastic charity that came into existence because of the group efforts of several individuals with the same values. One family found out that many kids with cancer have trouble making friends at school because their treatment can make them lose their hair, or the other kids are afraid to risk getting close to a child who might die. This inspired them to provide cancer victims with one week per year where they could come together with other kids just like them. Another family donated the land for the camp. The first week of camp was so successful the group immediately started trying to figure out how to provide another one. Twenty-five years later, the camp is open year-round, providing programs and gatherings not just for the children but for their families as well. From a few small individual gestures grew a program that has made a difference in thousands of lives.

What if your passion doesn't draw such an obvious link to a charitable organization? I had another client who loved cars; he was a real "motor head." More than anything, he wanted kids to learn about cars and get as excited about them as he was. After going through the A.S.K. process and talking to a few people, he realized that he could give kids a chance to learn more about cars by making it easy for them to visit his city's car museum. In the end, he set up a fund that would allow the museum to cover the cost of inviting school kids from underprivileged parts of town for a tour. The amount of money he had to offer wasn't a fortune, but with this small gesture, he was able to share something he loved and know that he had made a difference. This is another great example of how what starts in the Room of Dreams can move forward into the Legacy Room and on into the future.

Get Help

There's another conversation you should have once you've gotten a good sense of how you might want to build your legacy. You can use the information you've gathered to guide a dialogue with the professionals who can help you fulfill it, such as your accountant, estate attorney, or even your doctor. In essence, you want to build a brain trust. These people can help you evaluate your assets, from wealth to health, and advise you about some of the likely outcomes and possible implications of your decisions.

As in a real house, you want your Legacy Room to be well built, because every decision you make when you leave this room will be grounded in the discoveries you make here. You don't want to have to stop contributing to the organizations carrying your legacy, or for the other rooms in your house to crumble, because you didn't consult the right professionals or follow their advice. In addition, you want to be sure that you are allocating your money to charities that will use your contributions as intended and will guard your legacy wisely and responsibly.

The Legacy Room seeks to ensure that you will never look in the mirror with regret wondering what more you could have done. Next stop in the Your Financial House grand tour is the Lifestyle Room, where you're going to set your life up so that everything is in place to achieve the dreams and establish the legacy that means so much to you.

MAKE-READY

1. List at least five values for which you want to be known. What do you want people to think of when they think of you?

2. Note the ten relationships that you value most. Write down each person's name as well as how they are related to you (relative, neighbor, childhood friend, etc.).

3. Interview or send a questionnaire/link to an online survey to these people asking them to tell you what values they think you stand for. Be sure to ask for examples.

4. Which charities do you value the most? Write down not only their names but also their focus.

5. What religious organizations or affiliations do you value? Write down the names of those groups.

6. What other causes are important to you?

7. Now evaluate your lists. What are some common threads throughout your entries? How would someone else interpret your lists? After an honest evaluation, do you think your legacy lists are too short? How can you extend your influence? Have all this information handy the next time you meet with a financial planning professional.

Chapter Four

THE LIFESTYLE ROOM

Earlier we talked about how adults stop dreaming as big as they did when they were children because they start putting limitations on themselves. In other words, when challenged in the face-to-face showdown with reality, most people blink. And now here we are, in the Lifestyle Room, where we're about to get as real as we can get. That's right; we're finally going to look at some numbers. The ones on your credit card, to be exact, as well as in your bank account, on your pay stubs, on your mortgage statements, and in any other documents that lay out in black and white how much money you bring in and how much you spend. This is where we get the information that tells us how close you are to achieving your dreams and how well you are shaping your legacy.

Are you saying to yourself: "That's just cruel. What could possibly be the point of encouraging people to dream about their goals and legacy as though money were no object when, as the vast majority of us can attest, the numbers are going to show that they're a pretty big object after all?"

Are you sure about that?

You see, time and again clients come into my office convinced I'm going to take one look at their expenses and income, chastise them for living beyond their means, and then put them on a strict budget because there's no way in the world they're ever going to make their goals unless they live like church mice for the rest of their days. Well, I might do that if my job were exclusively to make my clients as much money as possible. But as we've established, while there's no doubt that making more money is a very good goal, you probably have other goals as well. Sometimes those goals require making more money, sometimes they don't. Therefore, my job isn't just to help you make more money; it's to help you reconcile the lifestyle you enjoy now with the lifestyle you want some day. And often, much to my clients' surprise, we find that the two really aren't very far apart at all.

Of course, sometimes there's a gap between them the size of the Grand Canyon! But that's okay too. The late great tennis champion Arthur Ashe said it best: "Start where you are. Use what you have. Do what you can." Considering the words came from a man whose outsized legacy belies the short time he had on this earth, I'd say that's pretty good advice.

So let's see where you are.

THE PUNCH LIST

In every new home construction project, the owner usually creates a punch list—that is, an inventory of generally small details that the developer or general contractor must complete before the homeowner will pay any remaining contract fees and declare the work officially finished. At this point in the Your Financial House process, you're going to complete your own punch list. Only when armed with all of the items on the list will you be ready to honestly assess how much money is coming in, how much is going out, and where it's going.

Punch List

During our meeting we will be discussing all aspects of your current financial situation, as well as your goals and objectives. In an effort to make this discussion more productive, I am providing the following list of documents for you to have at our meeting. Naturally, these documents will be treated confidentially.

Please have the following items available, where applicable, for each person:

[ ] Most Recent Payroll Stub

[ ] Business Arrangements
  [ ] Buy/Sell
  [ ] Deferred Compensation
  [ ] Stock Option or Bonus Plan

[ ] Personal Employment Benefit Statements
  [ ] 401(k), Pension Statement(s)
  [ ] Employee Stock Options
  [ ] Employee Stock Purchase

[ ] Federal and State Income Tax Returns

[ ] Wills and Trust Documents

[ ] Social Security Benefit Statements

[ ] Personal Asset Values
  [ ] Residence
  [ ] Vacation Property
  [ ] Land
  [ ] Rental Property
  [ ] Certificates of Deposit (CDs)

[ ] Insurance and Annuity Statements Contracts
  [ ] Life Insurance
  [ ] Disability Insurance
  [ ] Long-term Care Insurance
  [ ] Annuity Statements/Contracts

[ ] Bank and Investment Statements
  [ ] Savings Accounts
  [ ] Checking Accounts
  [ ] Brokerage Accounts

[ ] Contact Information
  [ ] Attorney(s)
  [ ] Accountant(s)
  [ ] Bank(s)
  [ ] Trustee(s)

[ ] Consumer Debt Statements
  (with interest rate information)
  [ ] Mortgage
  [ ] Automobile
  [ ] Credit Card
  [ ] Personal

If there is anything you feel we will benefit from knowing that is not listed above, please bring it with you to our meeting, so we can determine its relevance in our financial consulting process.* If you have any questions before our appointment, please contact our office.

*We do not provide legal, tax, or trust advice. For these types of services, please consult with your attorney or accountant.

After gathering all of the documents on your punch list, you'll have everything you need to start filling out your Lifestyle Assessment Form.

Your Lifestyle

your financial house
the blueprint for financial growth & security

INCOME

Description (company)	Owner (name, joint)	Income Type (salary, bonus, rent)	Annual Amount (Gross/Net)	Applicable Period (start/end dates)	Growth Rate

LIABILITIES

	Mortgage	Home Equity	Auto One	Auto Two	Personal	Credit Cards
Owner						
Principal						
Balance						
Interest Rate						
Payment Type (Int. only, P&I, etc)						
Payment Amount						
Amortization (number of years)						
Period (start/end date)						

Notes: _____
_____
_____
_____

For more information, visit yourfinancialhouse.com

I find that a lot of my clients tackle this step with a combination of excitement and dread. The truth is, the majority of people have only a vague idea where all their money goes, so the results of this assessment can be fascinating. ("We spend *how much* on food?") Yet I urge you to approach this as more than a mere annual checkup. Think of it as a full-body MRI that will reveal everything you need to know about the state of your finances. But unlike an MRI, we're not looking to differentiate between the good and the bad. Neither you nor anyone else should be making a judgment call; this is just about seeing what's there. So, whatever you do, don't get discouraged or embarrassed by what the numbers reveal. Remember, here in the Lifestyle Room we are doing so much more than just outlining your expenses and comparing them to your earnings. We want to figure out what allows you to enjoy life, because that has a huge impact on your mental and physical health. The better your mental and physical health, the higher your confidence and peace of mind, and the better your chances of fulfilling your Room of Dreams and Legacy Room plans. That's why as we build your financial house we will ultimately be looking for ways to make sure you continue to enjoy your lifestyle, not restrict it. So, by completing the Lifestyle Assessment Form, you are on your way to constructing a plan that is realistic and in line with your current lifestyle as well as to getting a glimpse into your future.

INTERPRETING THE NUMBERS

We all put gas in the car and pay the utility bills and buy groceries, but it's the things we do in addition to those obligations that define us and offer true insight into who we are. It means something if you discover your Lifestyle Room is filled with books or fishing reels or motorcycles (or all three). Or it might have a large section devoted to travel, restaurants, or club dues. Perhaps you love to spoil your nieces and nephews, so the "Gifts" column on your form boasts a particularly generous sum. These purchases and more—family vacations, greens fees, opera tickets, movies, shopping, football season tickets—are just some of the ways we choose to reward ourselves for doing well, and that we use to tell ourselves we're doing okay. Some people reward themselves a little too much or a little too often. In fact, most of the time people discover that these expenses make up a significant part of their spending each month.

My clients are always surprised, however, that when we see evidence of overspending I don't start wagging my finger and put them on a belt-tightening budget. That's because indulging in the things you love, even a little too much, is not a bad thing so long as it keeps you happy and motivated. A problem arises only when your spending starts to silently weigh you down with anxiety. It's when you look at your credit card statement every month, shake your head, and resolve to do better, only to fail time and time again. When that's happening, your indulgence isn't making you 100 percent happy and confident. Here in the Lifestyle Room, we're going to help you get to a place where it is.

So the first question to ask yourself once you've filled out your form is not "Can I afford this life?" but "Am I happy with this life?" Do you hear the difference? "Can I afford this life?" implies that you should feel guilty about some of your spending. Guilt is counterproductive. I want you to approach this exercise with an optimistic attitude that helps you make positive decisions. Don't jump to conclusions. It's too soon to tell whether you need to change your spending. You have to spend time in all of the other YFH rooms to confirm whether your lifestyle is putting the rest of your goals in jeopardy.

If your answer to the question "Am I happy with this life?" is "No," don't leave it at that. Make sure to articulate why. Usually the answer involves debt payments or demanding relationships. The good news is that the chapters that follow will help you explore how and why these problems are hurting your quality of life, and that will push you to think about solutions.

Good financial planning isn't about whittling down your life to the bare necessities; it's about figuring out how to find a healthy, productive balance between your needs and wants. Years ago, when I was a young financial advisor, I had a high-net-worth client decades older than I whom I respected a great deal. One day he surprised me by saying, "Greg, do you know who the two most important professionals in my life are, the ones that I'm counting on?"

Startled, I said, "Well, no sir, I don't."

He smiled. Then he said, "The first one is my doctor. He meets with me and tells me I shouldn't drink too much wine and I shouldn't have those big fat steaks with the baked potatoes, especially with lots of sour cream. And he tells me I should exercise more. That's my doctor's job, to give me advice—the knowledge I need to keep me going as long as I can. And most of the time, I follow it.

"You're the other important professional I rely on, Greg. You're the one that guides me, keeping me on the right track to help ensure I have everything I need to live for all the years my doctor keeps me going."

"But you know, I've got to eat a steak now and then. Sometimes I put sour cream on my baked potato. And as you know, I splurge a bit. But if we work together to build my wealth, those little extras won't keep me from passing it on. And remember, Greg, when I die the doctor's job is done, but your role goes on."

With the help of two professionals, this gentleman had designed a blueprint that enabled him to enjoy the occasional indulgence without ever sacrificing his long-term goals. His health, his wealth, and his dreams were secure, which allowed him to live life with confidence. The numbers staring at you right now are going to help you plan the blueprint that will help you do the same.

You might suspect that more often than not, the Lifestyle Assessment Form brings most people to the realization that they're spending too much money on little luxuries and need to drop them in order to save and retire comfortably. My friend David Bach, author of the mega-best-selling *Finish Rich* series, coined the phrase "The Latte Factor" to describe how dropping something enjoyable but unnecessary, like a daily latte, could add up to big savings down the road if you take the money you're not spending on coffee and invest it. I'm a huge fan of David's, but here I disagree with his idea that we need to eliminate all of the small luxuries of life in the interest of financial prudence.

What happens when most people go on a radical diet and eliminate all of the foods they love? They stop dieting because eating isn't fun anymore, and they get bored, and the deprivation makes them feel bad. The same goes with overly strict financial budgets. Of course you can save about four dollars a day if you stop buying that cup of coffee, but is the savings worth what you're losing in exchange? Officer Kevin Coffey (yes, his real name), an undercover Los Angeles police detective whose wife asked him to consider dropping his two-to-three-coffees-per-day habit during the Great Recession, explained the psychology perfectly to Howard Schultz, CEO of Starbucks, in an anecdote recounted in Schultz's book *Onward*. For Officer Coffey, it wasn't "just about a cup of coffee. I have a tough job. I see things every day that no one should see and experience. But the one good thing I can count on every single day is how the people in that store make me feel....This is my little escape."[2]

---

2. Howard Schultz, *Onward: How Starbucks Fought for Its Life without Losing Its Soul* (New York: Rodale, 2011), 191.

Life is meant to be enjoyed; we should not consider it a luxury when we hold on to the small pleasures that help us get through it. One person's luxury is another person's need, and that's what determines our lifestyle. So think about that when you're working on your budget.

Powell's Law #4: It's okay to have a latte.

The point of asking "Am I happy with this life?" is neither to find ways to restrict your lifestyle nor to push you into a more lavish one; it's just about finding the right lifestyle for you, the one that allows you to accomplish your dreams and legacy. Who knows, answering that question may even tell you that you're already there.

Case in point was a client who, after completing an YFH blueprint with her husband, clearly didn't believe what she was seeing. As we reviewed their plan, she kept looking down at her packet, then looking back at me, her eyes wide. Finally she interjected, "You mean, based on our lifestyle, and based on how much money we've set aside, we have college taken care of?" I assured her that their children's college futures were fully funded.

A few minutes later, she interrupted her husband to rephrase the question. "I am going to ask you one more time. You mean we can continue living the way we're living, and we have college taken care of?"

I chuckled, and promised that she needn't worry about college funds ever again. Because they had started early to save for college expenses, that plan had paid off. Their college fund concerns and related anxieties had been conquered. They had ample money to cover the children's higher education.

Her relief was striking. She had been living in a state of constant anxiety about how to pay for her children's education. She was ecstatic that the children were going to be fine, and that she and her husband could enjoy being empty nesters without continual sacrifice. Without realizing it, they had constructed the perfect Lifestyle Room for themselves.

This is yet another example of how a couple who has a dream to send their children to college can prepare to be able to afford to provide them with that great education and to see to it that those children will be debt free when they graduate. At the same time, that couple can have an enjoyable lifestyle. Sure, they would sacrifice if need be, but they needn't let life pass them by while putting their son and daughter through college. It shows how the Room of Dreams, the Legacy Room, and the Lifestyle Room all work together. Remember, the rooms of YFH are all connected.

I've been privileged to help people realize that they could retire anytime they wanted. I've seen people leave jobs they hate for less lucrative but more rewarding dream jobs. Because they had carefully constructed their Lifestyle Rooms, they could pursue those dreams with confidence.

LIVE THE LIFE YOU WANT

It would be terrible to be forced to abandon your dreams and goals because your lifestyle is hurting your quality of life or putting your retirement in danger. Sometimes you'll come to the conclusion that the only way to fulfill the benchmarks you set in the last two chapters is to make some adjustments, which could mean you wind up living a lifestyle that differs greatly from your friends' or that of the people with whom you work. It's important to be okay with that. Once you stop worrying about upholding any particular image, it becomes much easier to make the decisions that will help you furnish your Lifestyle Room in a way that lets you live the life you really want.

But what if, after reviewing your Lifestyle Assessment Form, you decide that certain dreams aren't worth the sacrifice they would require? That's fine, and you should make that choice with a clear heart. It's okay to go find another dream, so long as it's one that fulfills you. That's the key to happiness, no matter how much or how little money you have.

Money is nothing more than a building tool. Once you have completed your YFH blueprint, we will line up your dreams side by side with your finances and start figuring out the practical steps you will need to take to make them come true. We might decide that we need or want more tools. If that's the case, we'll keep it in mind as we move through the other rooms in the house and see what we can find for inspiration.

USE THE NUMBERS TO GUIDE THE CONVERSATION

If you share your home and finances with a partner or spouse, it's going to be as vital that you include that person in filling out your Lifestyle Assessment Form as it was to ask your significant other to contribute his or her thoughts in the Room of Dreams and Legacy Room.

This might not be the first time you two have sat down together to study your spending habits. Does this scenario sound familiar? One of you suggests to the other that it would be really smart if you put together a budget. A few weeks go by before you actually find a few minutes of quiet time to look at your credit card reports together. Within a few minutes, you point out how easy it would be to save a hundred dollars or so per month if your partner stopped buying lunch every day and brown-bagged it. Your partner, feeling defensive, retorts that it would be just as easy to save some money if you would quit going to that expensive gym. You both have reasons why these cutbacks are not good options. In the end, you finally agree to stop going to Sunday brunch so often and call it a day. But you haven't put any plan in place, so you both just keep spending, accruing increasing credit card balances, and hoping (praying) that somewhere down the line you'll make enough money to catch up.

This time, though, it's going to be different. In the Lifestyle Room, you're going to look at your expenses just as you always have, but now you're going to use your goals, dreams, legacies, and preferred lifestyles to guide your conversation. Simply scrimping or even working harder to make more money isn't going to raise your happiness level, either individually or as a couple. Working together to find money and putting it to work toward something you both want, however, is a wonderful way to strengthen your relationship.

Many times, I could almost see the stress sliding off client's shoulders as they discussed the Lifestyle Room. I find that often, a couple's time in the Lifestyle Room has opened up their communication channels and helped strengthen their relationship. Realizing this was a peak career moment for me. I realize many highly intelligent, successful people haven't been able to figure out for themselves how to break down their needs and wants. They need someone to ask the right questions and to facilitate their discussions about how to use their hard-earned money, and I am proud to be able to do that for them.

More Conversations

I've shown you examples of how couples have been able to use their time in the Lifestyle Room to better communicate and define their priorities, but they are not the only ones who can benefit in here. If you're single, widowed, or divorced, you may not have anybody to confide in or on whom you can test your ideas. You may not be confident that you're making wise decisions. But after defining your value-based priorities here in the Lifestyle Room, you'll be prepared to draft the rest of your financial blueprint, which you can then take to your financial advisor to confirm that you're on track.

WHAT'S THE MONEY MYTH?

The Money Myth is the belief that for every individual, there exists a dollar amount that leads to happiness. Generally, people who subscribe to the Money Myth believe there are only one or two paths to wealth: hard work and ideal investments. But, while it is true that hard work is key to succeeding in life—in fact, it's a cornerstone of the American Dream—these people often become slaves to it. They sacrifice their health, their friendships, and even their families for the next promotion or pay raise, which they believe will finally allow them to feel like they've made it to the top of the totem pole of life. This same mentality also often compels them to make risky investments in the hope that this time, their daring will pay off.

Do not believe the Money Myth. Yes, hard work is important, and good investments have the ability to pave paths to prosperity. But it is a myth—and a dangerous one, at that—to believe that working longer hours or pushing for the highest rate of return and taking risks with your family's financial future in pursuit of "more" is your best chance of achieving wealth or happiness. Don't live your life based on a myth, because the reality is that wealth and happiness are all about fulfilling your unique dreams and goals. With a YFH blueprint, you figure out how to best use what you've got—financially or otherwise—to help you pursue those goals so you're not exhausting yourself or stressing yourself out with the continual hunt for the elusive "more," because you'll know exactly how close you are to being able to sit back, smile, and enjoy "enough." Your time in the Lifestyle Room is key to getting on that track.

My hope is that you will feel confident and inspired by the time you're done in the Lifestyle Room. But, after taking such a close look at your spending habits and analyzing how much money goes out the door, you might feel relieved to move on to a room where you can examine what assets you possess that are bringing money in, or that have the potential to help fund your dreams.

Your Lifestyle Room will share a wall with your Wealth Room, which is which is where we are going to spend time next we are going to spend time in next. Keep the documents you rounded up for your punch list handy—you're going to need them.

MAKE-READY

1. Are you happy with the life you lead? What elements of your lifestyle give you the most pleasure?

2. What aspects of your life could be harmful to your relationships?

3. How healthy is your lifestyle? Does it allow you to enjoy your wealth?

4. What do you need to do to make sure that lifestyle is allowing you to fulfill your dreams, goals, and legacy?

5. Are there any changes you could make that would positively impact your budget without negatively affecting your life or morale?

6. After going through your Lifestyle Assessment Form, what have you decided will be the point at which you can happily say, "Enough!"?

Chapter Five

THE WEALTH ROOM

After reading the last chapter, you should have a clear understanding of your expenses, your income, and how well they're working together. If you're a numbers nerd like me, the title of this chapter might compel you to eagerly pull out your calculator, figuring this is where the fun starts. More often, however, I find that people come to the Wealth Room with a bit of trepidation, like my clients Sam and Joyce did. They became visibly uncomfortable when we got to this room. After hearing their story, I didn't blame them one bit.

Five years earlier they had worked with another advisor who had left them to organize all of their asset paperwork themselves before he would devise their financial plan. Gathering their papers had been an ordeal, and altogether it had taken about six months to get the actual plan done. In the end, Sam and Joyce went home with a huge binder filled with financial documents they couldn't decipher. And they never heard from their advisor again! By the time we met, the binder had been repurposed and was serving as an excellent doorstop in their master bedroom closet. They suggested to me that if I really wanted to look at their assets, they would be willing to lug the doorstop in. They clearly didn't want to dig through their papers again.

So many things disturb me about Sam and Joyce's story it's hard to know where to begin. But let me try.

First, it should never take six or even four months to draft a financial plan. If it does, it might be because your financial planner is charging by the hour.

Second, it should never be your job to organize your own financial documents. When choosing a financial advisor, find out how much of the work he or she will expect you to shoulder. At our firm, we do all of the work. That's why we give our clients the punch list you first encountered in the Lifestyle Room. In orderly fashion, it explains exactly what documents we're going to need to draft a financial blueprint. But we are very clear that we don't expect our clients to organize their papers for us. Mine can bring them in a plastic garbage bag for all I care (and they have). My colleagues and I know exactly what we're looking for, and we can dig up and copy the papers we need to put your plan together much faster than you probably could. Make sure your financial planner is not putting the organizational burden on you. Also, consider it a red flag if the advisor doesn't ask you for all of the documents listed on the punch list as well as the Wealth Room checklist, which follows later in this chapter. The person simply cannot do a quality job for you if he or she is not looking at your whole financial picture.

Finally, any plan that sits untouched for over a year has no long-term value. If your financial planner isn't calling to discuss updates, or if you aren't reviewing your plan periodically, your money may not be working for you the way it should. I asked Sam and Joyce to bring in their doorstop, but I also requested updated versions of the punch list documents they had already provided the first time around. Sam objected, saying they hadn't made any significant changes to their portfolio. Fortunately, I prevailed.

They brought in their doorstop and a new stack of papers, and together we went through every room in their house to design their blueprint. Two weeks later, I presented them with their completed plan. I also sat them down in front of their doorstop and their new plan to show them just how much their financial picture had changed over the past five years. In fact, because they hadn't regularly updated their plan, they had fallen behind on some of the goals they had set. It took only a little tweaking, however, to get them back up to speed.

In sum, a well-designed Your Financial House plan will never become a doorstop, and your visit to the Wealth Room need not be a time-consuming, exhaustive experience. Rather, it will allow you to:

- Perhaps uncover unexpected revenue
- Motivate you to get your possessions and treasures appraised, or to double-check that assets have been realistically valued
- Allow you to react quickly and decisively in the event of financial changes or crises while still protecting yourself and disseminating risk
- Identify what other financial professionals you need to bring in to your financial planning
- Make things easier for your loved ones if you're not around to tell them what you have

The work you do here in the Wealth Room will help you move forward toward fulfilling all of the plans you made in your Room of Dreams, Legacy Room, and Lifestyle Room. They are yours to protect. You'll have an organized document you can bring with you when you're ready to consult with a financial advisor, one that you can easily refer to and reevaluate every year. And in the end, you will not only have accurately identified and organized your wealth-building assets but also have ensured that every one of them is working for you.

HOW TO CALCULATE YOUR NET WORTH

Anyone should be able to calculate his or her net worth using this easy formula:

$$\text{Assets - liabilities = net worth}$$

Of course, you have to identify your assets and liabilities to plug into the equation. Let's take a closer look at each of those two categories.

ASSESSING YOUR ASSETS

The numbers we just examined in the Lifestyle Room are the noisy ones: that is, the ones that probably get a lot of attention because you have to keep up with them every month. But many other numbers don't make a lot of noise, preferring to sit quietly in the corner biding their time, happy to be ignored, slowly gaining in value yet not threatening you with late fees. These are your assets.

You might be someone who assumes it's easy to identify your assets. After all, you know what falls into this category of income because you put it there, consciously making purchases, investing, and depositing money in accounts that are designed to appreciate over the long term. Or maybe the opposite is true, and other than your home and your car, you know you have no assets.

As in the previous chapter, I have to ask: Are you sure about that?

You'd be surprised at the number of people I meet who don't know what they really own, much less what it's worth. They might be able to provide me with a list of their financial accounts, but they don't have a good grasp of the value of their overall portfolio. More than once, after going through the Wealth Room checklist, clients and I have discovered that certain assets hadn't been set up correctly and were either worthless or impossible to collect on. One gentleman I had known, for example, died in an accident, and when his widow tried to collect the insurance on his truck, she discovered he had never properly documented his truck registration. The asset was wasted.

You'd also be amazed at how many people I've worked with who claim to have few if any assets, only to discover after being prompted by their Wealth Room checklist that in fact they own jewelry, art, antiques, or even guns with far more than sentimental value. What this means is that it is absolutely worth your while to spend some time in the Wealth Room, because there is no other way to know for sure that you have accurately assessed your net worth. You can't build a financial house if you don't know what raw materials you have to work with.

Your list of assets should include anything that could possibly result in cash flow, whether in the form of dividends or interest, or as a result of a sale. Assets are either financial or physical. Your financial assets could include a 401K, a Roth IRA, or a SEP account; checking and savings accounts and pension funds; stocks, bonds, or mutual funds; copyrights and patents; even a life insurance policy. Your dad's mint antique train set, however, or your mother's signed first edition of *The Hobbit*, a vintage piece of Lalique, or an elaborate chandelier that turned out to be Waterford, an engagement ring, a stamp collection, a vacation property, as well as your home and your car—all of these would be considered physical assets. Below you'll find a basic Wealth Room checklist to help you list assets of both types.

Wealth Room

your financial house
the blueprint for financial growth & security

Description	Owner	Purchase/ Refinance Date	Purchase Amount	Previous Market Value	Current Market Value
Primary Residence					
Household Items					
Collectables					
Automobiles (Type/Year)					
Vacation Property					
Rental Property					
Land (Name of land)					
Business Interest					
Mineral Rights					

Notes: _____

_____

_____

_____

For a more detailed, extensive checklist to help jog your memory about assets you may not even realize you have, go to www.yourfinancialhouse.com.

Sometimes people complete a Wealth Room Assessment Form and question why there is no space to list an inheritance. I don't like to assume anything, and playing with phantom money will distort your true financial picture, which will be dangerous should that windfall not come to fruition. You may be absolutely certain an inheritance is in your future, but it would still be unwise to include that money in your financial blueprint until the funds are actually in your account. Analyze your net worth as is instead of counting on money or assets that may never appear.

Now, what about that signed first edition of *The Hobbit*? It's an incredible piece of literary history, it meant the world to your mother, and you would have to be on the brink of starvation to sell it. Can something so loaded with sentimental value really count as an asset if it's never going to be exchanged for cash? It can, because the banks that you might one day need to turn to for a loan don't care that you don't intend to sell that book. What matters is that the book exists, and that it's in your possession. All the banks want is an assurance that if they have to come after you for repayment of that loan, you've got the resources at your disposal. So start looking around your home. If you had a chance to appear on *Antiques Roadshow*, what would you bring?

It never hurts to get a potentially valuable item appraised, such as jewelry, antiques, land, rental real estate, and other assets. You'll not only gain more knowledge, you'll also be able to start educating the next generation to whom it will belong. Most important, you will get a clearer picture of your net worth. Clients have told me they had extremely valuable items in their possession, only to discover after visiting with an appraiser that they were almost worthless. It's always better to know the truth so you have a clear picture of your net worth and can plan for the future.

It's worth noting in this context that the Estate Planning Room is located above the Wealth Room. Part of the benefit of identifying your assets now is that it will also get you thinking about how you will want to pass these assets to the next generation. And it will be helpful to recognize that although your mother's copy of *The Hobbit* has incredible sentimental value to you, you can't predict whether it will hold the same value to a great-grandchild you've never met. Does that change to whom you think you might want to leave it? Would your children even know the value of this asset if you didn't identify and document it? If properly cared for, it could one day fund part of the next generation's education, or otherwise help them launch their lives and careers. If nothing else, identifying the book as an asset now will ensure that your heirs treat it with respect and care.

LIST YOUR LIABILITIES

Now let's turn to the category in the equation that you deduct from your assets. Your liabilities are, plain and simple, your debts. And unless you pay for everything in full and in cash, you've got them. Any credit card debts you owe, bank or college loans you need to repay, car payments you still need to make—those are all liabilities. Even your home, which you would naturally list as an asset, is also a liability until you've paid off the mortgage. Although this is a small section within *Better, Richer, Fuller*, it nevertheless plays a major role in the success of the YFH process. Too often, people don't want to look at this issue because they are scared their liabilities are out of control. They are afraid their debt problem cannot be repaired. Just like with a material house that suffers water or termite damage, the financial house you build can develop issues that cause you to be anxious. But guess what will happen if you do nothing? The house will eventually come tumbling down.

So, the first step you need to take is to address your liabilities by making a plan to solve them—to repair Your Financial House. And in doing so you'll soon discover that you've made this issue a bigger problem than it really is. Anxiety has taken over and you are embarrassed to discuss debts and liabilities. You aren't the first person to have such issues and you won't be the last. Start to A.S.K. questions about how you can solve your problems. Move forward with confidence and visualize Your Financial House with a strong foundation and walls.

KNOWING YOUR NET WORTH OPENS DOORS

As you can see, once you tally your assets and subtract from that figure your total liabilities, it should be extremely easy to know your net worth. But most people don't, even those who think they do. The reason is that most people tend to overestimate their assets and minimize their liabilities. It's just human nature. Here's a great story that illustrates my point.

I met with a gentleman who counted in his assets a house valued at 1.2 million dollars. He had made a number of big financial decisions based on the value of that house. However, he neglected to take into account that he had taken out an interest-only, five-year 1-million-dollar balloon mortgage on the home. That meant that in five years the loan would be due, yet there was no guarantee that in five years he would be able to sell the house for the same amount or more than he had paid for it. Without that liability on his balance sheet he seemed to be a very wealthy man, but the real numbers revealed that he did not have much of a net worth.

Wait! He also pointed out to me that he owned a business. That was an asset, wasn't it? Well, yes, on the surface it looked like one, but digging deeper we saw that his business had debts and sales were going down each month. This was a family business that had been passed down through three generations, and my client had assumed that because it had always been successful it would continue to be so. By working through the YFH process a person comes to realize the true value of what they have. Appearances do not pay the bills or provide a life of happiness.

This is why it's so important to meet with a professional financial advisor once you've drafted your financial blueprint. You need someone with an objective eye to take a look at the values you've placed on your assets and liabilities lists and to make sure you're not overlooking anything or inadvertently under- or overestimating the numbers.

While it's eye-opening to figure out your net worth, the real purpose of the Wealth Room is to prompt you to think hard about your assets, to collect the documentation you'll need to prove their value, or to get them documented if you haven't already so you're ready to have a productive dialogue with your advisor once you've walked through the other rooms in Your Financial House. Whether you figure out your net worth now or let your advisor calculate it for you later, knowing that number will serve you in many ways.

Knowing your net worth can help any advisor you work with create a customized financial advisory board. For example, financial planners might be responsible for managing all of their clients' money, but they are likely not tax specialists. Therefore, if they notice that clients are paying an inordinately large amount of proceeds to Uncle Sam, their financial advisor should be able to contact the client's CPAs (with the client's per-mission, of course) to discuss what arrangements can be made to better safeguard that money.

The YFH process takes financial advice and services to a whole new level because it coordinates all of the contributions from the pertinent professionals and motivates them to communicate. It helps the client see the importance of that communication, which in turn can give the client more opportunities to potentially increase his or her net worth by making prudent decisions. For example, it's in the client's best interest for a financial advisor to keep an estate attorney abreast of any changes the advisor makes to the client's investments to ensure that those changes don't inadvertently alter arrangements the client has made in his or her will. Just as all of the parts of your life are connected, all of the parts of your financial life are connected, from the way you set up your estate to how you title property to the names you list on an account. In any business, various departments each have their own domain and responsibilities, but they also work together, checking, balancing, and supporting each other to make sure the business is run as smoothly and efficiently as possible. All of the financial and legal professionals in your life should be united in the goal of protecting and growing the business of you. When they aren't, terrible mistakes can happen, as the following story illustrates.

I recently met with a mother and one of her two sons. The patriarch of the family had passed away unexpectedly. Both children were grown with families of their own, but just the one son was working with his mother in the family business. After her husband's death, the mother had worked with another financial advisor to title some investments in her and her son's names so that if she herself became incapacitated or hospitalized, the son would have access to the money and be able to write checks. Unfortunately, as we discovered after going through the assets she listed in the Wealth Room, the bank had assigned them joint tenancy with rights of survivorship. This did indeed give the son authority to write checks on behalf of his mother, but if she died, his brother would be cut out of those investments, even though the mother's will asserted that both sons would share equally in all parts of her estate. In addition, the joint tenancy meant that should the mother cause an accident and be sued, the plaintiff could come after her son for damages, too.

Because there had been no communication between the estate planner and the former financial planner, neither professional recognized he was putting the family in a potential predicament. This illustrates why our work in the Wealth Room is not just about identifying where we can make more money using your assets; it is equally about harnessing other professionals' expertise and double-checking that your assets are working together to your benefit and the benefit of your heirs.

As for the mother and her son, their story had a happy ending. We started the Your Financial House process and walked them through each of the rooms. Once we had drawn up their YFH blueprint, we arranged a lunch meeting that would include the two of them as well as their estate attorney, corporate attorney, CPA, and insurance agent. It was the first time everyone had gathered in the same room. Respectful that the professionals in the room where charging for their time, we had created an efficient agenda using topics from the YFH blueprint. Within the allotted two hours, we addressed all of the issues and assigned each of the professionals the relevant part of the blueprint they were to complete.

If an advisor tells you it is not his or her habit to consult with other professionals you've retained, look elsewhere for financial planning guidance. Everyone deserves to receive this kind of care and respect from the individual they've charged with the important task of helping them lay out a financial life plan. Only when you and your financial advisor study your financial life as a whole, examining all of its disparate parts, will you both have the information you need to refurnish or rearrange your Wealth Room.

For instance, it may turn out that because most of your assets are in real estate or in an employer's stock, you've put yourself at significant risk. Or, as you passed from earlier stages in your life, which are usually the wealth accumulation years, to later stages, which are more often the distribution years, you may have neglected to make changes to your holdings. Or, you may realize that the property you inherited has never been properly valued. It might prove to be of real worth, but then again, it might prove to be a real liability. You'll need to consult with an insurance agent, a lawyer, or a tax advisor to determine which. Everything must be evaluated and reevaluated so that you can draft a reliable blueprint for your future. Your advisor should be like a home staging specialist who takes an objective walk-through of your Wealth Room to help you realize the full value of what you have and to point out which possessions might be hurting the overall value of your house.

PREPARE FOR THE UNEXPECTED

Knowing your assets inside and out will ensure that they are all working for you. But have you realized that knowing your assets inside and out could potentially help protect you from downturns and allow you to make quick decisions when the unexpected arrives?

I received a frantic phone call one day from my client Mr. Smith. In a panic, he blurted that his parents had just called him to admit they needed money to pay their bills. He wanted me to make arrangements to withdraw the funds he assumed he'd have to pull out of his and his wife's pending retirement account to care for his parents.

Mr. Smith and I were familiar with all of the assets in his and his wife's Wealth Room, but neither of us had any idea what was in his parents'. So before we started withdrawing any money, I suggested we meet with his parents and tour their financial house. We did, and drafted a financial blueprint for them that better utilized the assets we found in their Wealth Room.

Ultimately, rather than allowing the younger generation to rush to the rescue by writing a check that risked their own ability to retire, we were able to come up with a sustainable plan. I was so glad the two generations of Smiths had been willing to let an objective professional ask the right questions and help them find alternative answers.

STRENGTHS ARE ASSETS TOO

In another instance where the Wealth Room offered an opportunity to an unexpected event, a woman named Tricia came to see me following her divorce. She hadn't worked outside her home for ten years, and she was anxious about how she was going to support herself. We started working on her financial house, beginning, as always, in the Room of Dreams. There she told me she had always enjoyed painting religious artwork and canvas art that appealed to teenagers. She had given her work to family members and friends for birthdays and holidays, only to get calls from *their* friends and colleagues for her artwork. As we assessed her strengths, it became apparent that she was a very creative, talented artist with a long list of ideas she had been sitting on for years. Buoyed and inspired by the A.S.K. process, which had given her the knowledge she needed to quell her anxieties and regain her sense of control, she went home and made about five sample items. She wrote a business plan and scheduled an appointment with a large retailer, to whom she presented her five sample products and her business plan.

At the end of that presentation, one of the representatives said, "We want these five products in one hundred of our stores next fall." Upon hearing those words, Tricia immediately panicked. But she managed to swallow, smile, and sign a contract. Then she called me.

Together with my colleagues, we asked the questions that helped her gather the knowledge she needed to fulfill the contract. She presented the contract to a bank, securing a line of credit. She used that line of credit to send her product to China, to be reproduced by a manufacturer. The Chinese manufacturer got the stock back in time for the stores to receive their orders. Now Tricia is the owner of a thriving business, including multiple product lines.

Do you see where I'm going here? Indirectly, the strengths you identified back in the Room of Dreams should also be counted among your assets, even though they don't necessarily have tangible monetary value. Tricia's success came about as a result of recognizing that one of her strengths, her creativity, was also an asset. A bank may not value these "soft" assets, but you should. They are as much a part of your wealth as stocks and bonds, real estate, or pension funds are.

Another strength we often overlook is being in good health. It is an asset as valuable as any of your possessions because it allows you to continue increasing your overall wealth. Conversely, poor health can be a liability because it limits how much you can work to increase or even just enjoy the wealth you already have.

Powell's Law #5: A health issue can be a wealth issue.

The A.S.K. process that highlighted Tricia's strengths is an excellent system for finding ways to refill a Wealth Room that has been depleted or otherwise left sparsely furnished. After one client died of a stroke at age forty-three, his widow suddenly found herself assuming the full responsibility of sending their three children through college. She didn't want to burden those children with large student loans, but this crisis meant the Wealth Room she had created with her husband wouldn't be funded as intended. So we looked for other solutions, including universities with special programs, scholarships, and other resources. By identifying her strengths (which included having smart kids, each with a strong work ethic, for example) and gathering the knowledge she needed, this financial house owner was able to add to her Wealth Room and tweak her blueprint to adapt to the unexpected changes in her life.

GROW YOUR WEALTH

While one of the main directives for a financial blueprint is to preserve any wealth that already exists, it should also create opportunities to let that wealth grow. So, you have to think about where you want your wealth to come from. Is it enough if it just stems from your savings? What about making some investments beyond your retirement account? Could you buy commercial real estate, timberland, or beach properties? What about the stock market?

One thing I hear often is people expressing a desire to start their own business, in which case knowing the contents and value of their Wealth Room inside and out could give them a major advantage. Because a business owner who has completed her Wealth Room, finished building her whole financial house, and lined up the professionals needed to keep that house well maintained and secure will have all of the knowledge she requires to make the decision of whether or not to sell, and if so, for how much. It gives her an opportunity to build a business that is working for her, not the other way around. (If it's working for you—if it can continue and increase in value without you at the helm—you've got a business; if not, you've still got just a job.)

Remember Jerry in the first chapter, who launched his own business? He thought his layoff was a personal and professional disaster. But if he had categorized his assets and gained a comprehensive understanding of his total net worth beforehand, he would have immediately seen the early out as the opportunity to fulfill his dreams that it really was instead of temporarily collapsing with despair. He did all right for himself in the end, but it would have been far less painful if he'd been able to respond more like my client Gary did when he received similarly unexpected news.

A key executive in his company and an expert in his field, hospital construction, Gary learned one day that his company wanted him to relocate. When he shared the news with his wife and children at the dinner table that night, they looked at him incredulously. They didn't want to leave their home or community. And as he watched their reactions, he realized he didn't want to either.

Fortunately, Gary had built a solid financial house and drafted a financial blueprint. In his Room of Dreams, he had noted that one day he would love to open his own business. And his Wealth Room revealed a respectable list of assets. Armed with that knowledge, he approached us for help developing a business plan. We were able to support him as he walked through the Small Business Administration loan process and worked with a local bank that handles such loans to set up his company. He then used the cash flow from his successful business to help pay back the loan. Thanks to having done such a thorough analysis of the contents of his Wealth Room, Gary is now happily pursuing the career mapped out in his Room of Dreams, and he and his family are still enjoying dinner together in the same home.

Building a financial house is not just about preserving what you've got; it's also about finding out what opportunities are out there to grow it. But unless you reevaluate your Wealth Room every year, you'll never really know what you have, because assets appreciate and depreciate. In order for your blueprint to work, you have to know at all times whether your net worth is increasing or decreasing. Once you know how all your net worth is tied together, you and your advisor can have a realistic discussion about any refurnishing, rearranging, or removing that needs to be done as you strive to make your assets work better, protect you from downturns, and increase your profitability.

Knowing the contents of your Wealth Room and knowing that you've done everything you can to make it work for you is empowering. You're like Dorothy at the end of the yellow brick road: you find out that you had the tools—your shoes—to get home all along; you just didn't know how to make them work. The Wealth Room holds all of the numerical data any financial advisor could use to build a portfolio, but when combined with the insights you've gained from the Room of Dreams, the Legacy Room, and the Lifestyle Room, it can help clear a path towards success and security. It's a room that encourages you to consider the numerous ways you can seek to preserve and grow your wealth using what you've got.

The next room we're about to visit will give you a chance to consider how you might be able to create some brand-new additional revenue streams. If you'll just follow me...

MAKE-READY

1. Organize and evaluate all of your assets. Did you discover any that surprised you?

2. Are the items within your Wealth Room structured so that you can make adjustments when the unexpected happens?

3. Do you need help completing your Wealth Room? First, make sure you go to yourfinancialhouse.com and print off the Punch List, which will give you a Wealth Room section to complete. It will help jog your memory and focus your attention on your net worth. List your assets and liabilities. Also, talk to your CPA and your current financial advisor. Remember, having your financial team in place is important to the YFH process and to your success! If so, start getting recommendations for a professional who can help you get organized.

Chapter Six

THE FINANCIAL OPPORTUNITY PROFILE ROOM

Welcome to the second floor of the Your Financial House process. I am excited to continue the tour. Like climbing a staircase, the YFH process takes you through each room step by step, and even takes you to a higher level as you advance in learning more about all of the details you need to know in building your financial house and your future.

By now, many financial books would be discussing investment products that you need to place your money in for growth or income. My belief is that you don't even need to go to those products until your financial house has been fully designed and your questions have been answered. Yes, there are many different ways and many types of investments you can choose from as you work to increase your wealth over time. Before you invest, however, you need to know the meaning of risk level and your risk tolerance. That is why the Financial Opportunity Profile Room is next. It is here where you discover the minimum rate of return you need in order to achieve your lifetime goals.

Indulge me a minute, please. I know the Financial Opportunity Profile name lends itself to becoming the acronym the "FOP Room," which is easy to remember. Go ahead. But FOP is important on another level in this discussion. The original fifteenth-century Middle English noun "fop" (based on the verb "to deceive") meant a foolish or silly person. I love this, because the Financial Opportunity Profile Room is all about "risk," and too often, foolish or silly investors will take too much risk or not enough risk and totally destroy their financial future. Spend time in the FOP room now to avoid being a fop in your future.

Let me ask you a question: If you had to choose between your money outperforming the Standard & Poor's (S&P's) 500 index* or your money growing to achieve your dreams and goals, which option would you choose? In my thirty-plus years of advising people, *no one* has ever chosen outperforming the S&P 500 index; *everyone* has selected having their money grow to achieve their dreams and goals. That is the very reason why the FOP Room exists. If you can achieve your dreams and goals for the least amount of risk, then quit trying to speculate with your money. In other words, your investment strategies should try to get you the best investment return possible for the least amount of risk. Don't be a fop who tries to get rich quick by taking risks that might not work out.

So, think about it. In each room you've visited so far in your financial house, you made an assessment. First you assessed your dreams and goals (Room of Dreams). Then you went to rooms where you assessed who you are (Legacy), how you live (Lifestyle), and what you have (Wealth). Thus, it would make sense to think that with a name like the Financial Opportunity Profile Room, this next room is where we stop assessing and start taking some action. Perhaps by discussing some good investments that will help you set your sights on making the most money possible—you know, looking for those financial opportunities.

But that's not why I called this the Financial Opportunity Profile Room. Its name actually refers to the fact that your finances should give you the opportunity to live the life you want. The thing is, though, too much or too little risk could take that opportunity away. So we need to make another assessment, this time of the amount of risk you've taken on. It matters because it's the amount of risk you will take with your money, even more than the amount of money you will make, that often will make all the difference in whether you fail or succeed in reaching your goals.

Powell's Law #6: Risk is the determining factor that brings up or breaks down our net worth.

In this room, you'll find out whether your assets are really working for you the way you think they are, and you'll make sure they are balanced so that you're earning enough to reach your goals and dreams, to build your legacy, and to support your lifestyle—while minimizing your risk.

REALITY CHECK

You may not think you need a reality check, but everyone does. You can look like a millionaire headed down a quick path to your dreams in the Wealth Room, only to discover here, in this room, that you've actually got a long road ahead.

A number of years ago I had a client who was making well over $200,000 and had in excess of $1 million in stock. But that stock was all in one company—the one she worked for. I implored her to diversify her assets, but the company's stock had gone through the roof, and, never having made that kind of money before, she didn't want to leave a dime on the table. She told me not to worry: she knew her industry and had her finger on the pulse of her company; she'd be the first to know when the market had hit its peak. Unfortunately, a new technology was introduced that rapidly undermined her industry. The company's stocks plummeted and sales dried up. Almost overnight, the company declared bankruptcy, and my client lost everything. You have to build your financial house on a solid foundation. Yet, despite my warnings, this woman insisted on building hers on a flood plain.

You could chalk this story up to an exceptional case of hubris, but I assure you, this woman was not the only Icarus who flew too high that year. This is an excellent example of the dot-com bubble that occurred in the late nineties. There is no doubt that this lady got too close to the dot-com sun shining in her face, with its blinding vision of pots of gold. People get giddy and shortsighted when their investments are going well because most have been told that it's the amount of money they have that matters. But with investments, a bird in the hand isn't always worth more than two in the bush. What if the bird you've got is secretly sick and dying? Or, unbeknownst to you, it has been spotted by a predator? If the money you have is vulnerable to risk, it's not worth nearly as much as you think it is.

The same can be said if you don't take enough risk. After all, flying too low to the ground can be just as dangerous as flying too near to the sun. I meet with couples all of the time that have sacrificed for years to fill their savings accounts, but they never invested their money to really see it potentially grow and gain. When my team projects their savings needs and informs these couples they're probably going to be out of money by age seventy-five, they are astounded. Risk intolerance regarding investments can make you as bad off as the highly risk-tolerant speculator.

Just remember this: extreme risk in investments—being either too highly speculative or too conservative—can cause disruptions in your own financial house.

Not only do you need to start thinking about how to keep your money safe, you also need to start thinking about how to make it grow at a pace that will provide you with the funds you need to furnish the other rooms you've established through the Your Financial House process. If you concentrate on safety and growth instead of on how quickly you can make money or how much money you can hoard, you will be on your way to constructing a solid financial house. You'll have what you need. Of course, if all goes well, you could potentially earn more than you need. It will be gravy, as the saying goes: that is, enough to make things extra delightful and to prevent you from having to worry that it could all disappear.

Such extra funds might be important, especially because spending patterns in retirement don't always match what academic studies predict they'll be. Many online formulas, for instance, will assure you that you need only 80 percent of your current income, assuming your expenses will go down. I don't think that's true. In my clients' experiences, the first five years of retirement are often their most expensive. That's when they write big checks for their romantic trip to Europe or their whole-family celebratory cruise. If you have carefully maintained the Your Financial House blueprint you created, those big checks can be wonderful investments, fulfilling what you've planned in your Room of Dreams and the Legacy Room. Those first five years can be some of the most fulfilling of your life.

WHERE TO LOOK FOR RISK FACTORS

There are three areas in your life where too much or too little risk can wreak havoc on your financial house: Your investments. Your business or job. Your relationships.

All three of these areas involve emotional ties. As a result, people often move too quickly to make a decision in any one of them based on emotion rather than facts. I cannot emphasize enough how important the FOP Room is to your financial planning. Let's look at each area in detail to make sure you understand and are comfortable with your level of risk concerning your investments, your business or job, and your relationships.

Assess Your Investments

In the Wealth Room, my client who lost her nest egg appeared to be a high-net-worth person, even though the Financial Opportunity Profile Room showed otherwise. It's crucial that you assign realistic values to the assets you listed in your Wealth Room. Just as they are, those assets will be valuable if you ever need an influx of cash or collateral; it's the combination of income, cash, and growth, however, that will get you to your retirement goals.

So the first thing you will need to do is calculate how much money you will need to reach them. Well, that's easy, right? Just pull up one of those online calculators offered on almost every financial website and plug in the numbers, such as how much you earn, how much you've saved, and how much you think you'll draw from home equity.

Unfortunately, it's not that easy. A more realistic formula for calculating how much money you'll need to earn to achieve your goals upon retirement is this:

**Desired annual income ÷ .04 = Total dollars you will
need to generate desired annual income**

Whenever I ask people how much money they'd need to earn upon retirement to live the way they'd like to, some say $100K, some say $200K, and some have grown accustomed to a lifestyle that would require even more. Regardless of your magic number, the calculation is the same. Plug $100K into the formula above and you'll find that you'll need $2.5 million, generating 4 percent earnings, to attain it. Someone needing $200K would need about $5 million, generating 4 percent earnings, and so on and so forth.

Two million dollars is a lot. If you don't already have it, how are you going to earn it? Well, one way is to set more aside and cut back somewhere, or make a career choice that will get you into a higher income bracket. But before taking that step, let's look at your accounts. How can you get the most realistic assessment of their value? How can you find out how vulnerable they are to risk? Some people simply open a 401K or Roth IRA and ignore it until the day they retire; they may never actually talk to the companies managing them. But you should. Call or e-mail and ask the company for their projections at the current rate of return. How you manage your 401K or any other retirement account could make all the difference in how well you do down the road.

The traditional buy-and-hold-and-hold-and-hold strategy that dominated the financial planning industry for years might not be profitable in an era when markets react almost instantaneously to events around the world, causing drastic fluctuations. You need to build a firm financial foundation that takes multiple scenarios into account. That's how you work to optimize the upside of the market while protecting your downside. But you can't do that if you don't know where you're vulnerable to risk, and most people don't know where to look for it.

Here are some of the biggest mistakes people make when calculating their net worth:

Overestimating your rate of return: Human nature being what it is, most people consistently overestimate their rate of return. Most online calculators offer you the choice of earning 6, 8, or 10 percent on your investments, but that's pie-in-the-sky thinking. If it were so common for people to earn 10 or even 8 percent on their investments, we'd have a lot more millionaires living next door.

Competing against the S&P 500: Remember the S&P 500 question I asked you at the beginning of this chapter? Indulge me, please, as I ask you again and elaborate on it in relation to financial advisors. If you had to choose between your money outperforming the S&P 500 index or your money achieving your dreams and goals, which would you pick? In my thirty-plus years of financial advising, no one, not even professional mutual fund managers, has ever said they'd prefer to outperform the S&P 500. Everyone, without exception, wants to achieve his or her dreams and goals more than anything else. So you have to wonder, why do so many financial advisors brag about their performance against the S&P 500 to prove their mettle? Shouldn't they be bragging about their success rate in helping their clients reach their financial goals?

There have been entire decades, such as between 2000 and 2010, in which you would have had a negative overall return if you had been in the S&P 500 index. How would you have felt about that if you were a retiree dependent upon that income? Or imagine yourself meeting with a financial advisor in 2008 who crowed: "Hey, great news! We performed better than the S&P 500 index!

It was down 40 percent, but we were only down 35 percent!" You wouldn't feel much like celebrating.

Too many people in the financial industry are using the wrong benchmarks to measure success. Think about that if you manage your own financial accounts, and especially any time you consider choosing or continuing business with a financial advisor.

Underestimating your life span: It's not enough to merely save for retirement; you'll need to produce both income and growth during retirement. Why? You might live longer than you think. We are now seeing a generation that has been retired as long as they were in the workforce. Thanks to advances in medicine and healthier lifestyles, insurance actuaries are now projecting life spans to age 110. I tell everyone that they should project their financial needs to age 100. And that's not a new practice. Today I have clients in their 80s and 90s who started working with me when they were in their 50s and 60s. Most of them laughed when I told them all those years ago that we would project their needs to age 100. No way would they see their hundredth birthday. And yet, here they are.

Limiting your investments: This one is simple: no matter how confident you—or your brother-in-law, or your golf partner, or your office mate, for that matter—are in a particular stock, tying up a vast portion of your net worth in only one or two investments is a supremely imprudent decision. You must also realize the necessity of knowing what the average rate of return is that you need to achieve your dreams and goals. The next time a family member or coworker gives you a hot stock tip, look at the person and say, "You know, I really appreciate your tip, but I think it would create too much risk in my portfolio. I'm on track to reach all of my financial goals and I just don't need to speculate with my money." Don't let the fear of not being rich enough overcome your confidence of being on track to live the lifestyle you want.

Assess Your Business or Job

Small businesses, defined as companies with fewer than five hundred employees, make up 99 percent of all of the businesses in the United States according to the 2012 US Census Bureau. Given those statistics, there's a really good chance many of the readers of this book own one. And of all of the people I meet who might indulge in too much risk, you're one of the more likely ones. Individuals blessed with an entrepreneurial spirit are just more willing to put everything on the line in return for potential gain. Most of the time that spirit serves you well. But there are two things every small business owner should keep in mind while in the Financial Opportunity Profile Room:

Your business is your aggressive investment.

If you're like most business owners, you're probably hoping that one day down the road someone within your company will buy you out, or that you'll be able to sell your company, or that you can transition the company to family members. Your business might represent a major portion of your portfolio. That makes sense. But then there's the rest of the portfolio. Because many entrepreneurial business owners are more comfortable with risk than the average investor is, they can have a tendency to gravitate toward aggressive-growth stocks. What they don't realize is that they already have an aggressive-growth stock—their business. To protect themselves, the rest of their portfolio might be limited to conservative or, at the very least, only moderately risky investments.

Your business shouldn't be your only investment.

I met with a couple that owned some franchises of a publicly traded company. They also owned stock in the parent company that franchises the businesses. This meant that if something were to happen to their franchises or if the economy tanked on the retail sector, they would be totally exposed. And both were in their 60s! I was surprised they'd take such a major risk. No one should be so highly concentrated in one type of asset that their wealth could be wiped out by one economic downturn, especially a couple so relatively close to retirement.

In addition, here are some tips everyone should follow, whether they own a business or merely work for one.

> **Stay alert and be aware of trends:** Even if you don't actually own a business, you need to be aware of the cycles and sensitivities of your industry. Howard Schultz, CEO of Starbucks, publicly called on Congress to get its act together when gridlock threatened to shut the government down. Why? Because when gridlock threatens the government, consumer confidence goes down and people stop buying affordable luxuries like coffee. But it's not just the CEOs of companies that need to stay vigilant. If you work for Starbucks, what happens in the markets can affect your job, too. If you work for the oil and gas industry, you could be affected by decreasing fuel prices. If you work for an ice cream chain, and the whole world decides to go Paleo, it could be a problem. Know your product lines. Are they sensitive to downturns in the economy? Are you prepared to adjust your portfolio to alternate between risk and caution as necessary? If you're in a career that can have high turnover or gets hit quickly in the event of economic slumps, like advertising or retail, your investment strategies necessarily need to be more conservative than you might wish them to be, just to make sure you're protected at all times.

Don't let money get in the way of making money: Sometimes people have a tendency to get hung up on things that just don't matter that much. Fees, for example. I have met people who have chosen a poor-performing investment over an outstanding one simply because the weaker investment didn't require a fee. Look, I agree that money is money and it shouldn't be wasted, and that no one should pay outrageous fees. Look at fees as well as performance when making any investment decision.

There are plenty of other investments that offer liquidity and won't cost you so much up front. But don't be obsessed with avoiding fees. Sure, you can invest elsewhere and save a few thousand dollars overall; but the difference between a high-fee investment and a low-fee one may be as great as the difference between a junk car and a Lexus. They both have four wheels and an engine, but only one is really likely to actually get you to your intended destination.

Some people become fixated on avoiding paying taxes too. I've met people poised to make a substantial return by selling and taking profits who balked because they didn't want to pay the taxes due. A little time passes and suddenly there's a downturn and all of their profits evaporate. Don't let an aversion to taxes or fees dictate your financial planning decisions.

Assess Your Relationships

Most of us recognize that our spouses will have some effect on our financial futures. If one of you gets laid off, that's going to have an impact on both of you. So will an inheritance or an illness. But that's the point of hitching our wagon to someone else's, right? We are publicly stating our intent to stand by our partner and face Real Life together, for better and for worse. Though there is nothing we can do to prevent most of the real-life situations that might unexpectedly affect our finances, there is something we can do to make sure our spouse or significant other is on the same page we are.

Unfortunately, the one thing that many people just don't do before they say "I do" is talk about money. Yet often it's financial disagreements that ultimately derail a marriage. In fact, a 2012 study showed that among all of the issues new married couples argued over, from children to sex to in-laws, those couples that argued about money were the most likely to be divorced two to five years later.[3] Even if you don't divorce, if you're a conservative investor married to someone with a taste for risk, your future could be jeopardized unless you make sure to build trust and can mutually agree on a financial plan. Your relationships will have a significant impact on the ultimate state of your portfolio.

I met Bill and Theresa the morning after an eventful dinner they had had at home. Bill had just put a forkful of food in his mouth when his tearful wife announced that she had been day trading without his knowledge. Convinced she could turn an eventual profit, Theresa had risked more and more for months. By that evening she had lost $150,000 on margin. Bill told me he took the fork out of his mouth, set it on his plate, and without a word to Theresa, picked up his phone and contacted a friend who was a client with our firm to ask how he could get in touch with our group. It was going to take a lot of work to repair their finances and their marriage.

Don't worry if you've been married twenty years to someone with a completely different philosophy toward money than you have. All is not lost—and you've apparently been doing a lot of things right. But you could mitigate your risk if you confront this difference and commit to working out a financial plan that acknowledges it. For example, together

---

3. Kansas State University "Early financial arguments are a predictor of divorce", Science Daily, 12 July 2013, http://www.sciencedaily.com/releases/2013/07/130712102438.htm.

you might consider making larger contributions from your paychecks to your 401Ks or IRAs so there is less money for the heavy spender of the couple to "play" with. Or you might cancel all but one credit card and share it between you so that one of you has to take the step of asking the other for the card before making any purchases over, say, $50.00. (That's a solution that will probably become obsolete when we're all paying for things with our phones, but it could be a training stopgap for now.) Your conversations shouldn't just be about fixing anyone's saving and spending habits; they should also be about making sure your lines of communication are open and that you're both working toward the same goals. Brainstorming possibilities to help you achieve those goals ahead of time will help facilitate your conversation when you eventually meet with a financial planner, and your ideas will help him or her guide you toward the best solution for you both.

What if you're not married? Have you ever stopped to think about how your extended family might affect your financial life down the road? Who will take care of your elderly aunt if her brother, your father, dies before she does? How about your siblings? What if you have a sister with special needs, and you know your parents couldn't have set nearly enough money aside to last her lifetime? You need to realize that you're not retiring for one, but for two. If your life is in any way entwined with another—and whose isn't?—what happens to that person, and the choices he or she makes, could potentially affect your financial future. Better to give that possibility some thought now rather than get blindsided down the road and feel pressured into making hasty, possibly financially irresponsible decisions.

And if you've got children, you've got a lot of thinking to do, even if they're already grown and out of the house. They are a blessing, but they are also your biggest investment and your biggest risk. They could set their heart on a college that costs far more than you budgeted for. They could give you a grandchild who needs expensive medical treatments, and you'll want to contribute. You could have sons or daughters who all fly away and have stellar careers and never ask you for a penny, but the reality is that life isn't always easy. How much will you be willing to risk to help them? Would that amount sacrifice your own goals? Once you've thought through these questions, you'll be ready to walk into the room right next door, the Children's/Heirs' Room, where you can start working on mitigating the risk that you'll ever be faced with such a dilemma.

ASSESSING RISK HELPS REMOVE THE EMOTION

A few years into his retirement a client of mine got bored with his daily golf routine and called me to make this startling announcement: "I've decided to go in with a few of my golf buddies and build a golf course."

I asked what he knew about developing a golf course. He replied that he played golf every day. I told him the truth: without a careful analysis of that sector and his own assets, he would be taking an enormous risk with his hard-earned wealth. But he was excited, and he had already made up his mind. He ignored my counsel.

You can guess the rest of the story. This individual drained all of his life savings trying to develop a golf course that never opened. Last I heard, he had lost not only all of his financial assets but also his marriage of fifty years. He was living in another person's home. Because he refused to calculate risk, he lost everything and everyone dear to him.

Now, it's not that a golf course might not be a good investment under different circumstances. But make sure you go in with the odds in your favor by assessing your risks ahead of time. The thought process of assessing your risks is invaluable. It will help you compensate if your partner's spending, saving, or investment habits don't match yours. It will keep you from caving in to hype and making irresponsible investments. It will help you seek solutions for a wayward grandchild without risking your financial future. It will help you readdress speculative investments during a career downturn.

Calculating risk is an ongoing process, so make the decision now that every year you will return to this room to reevaluate your risk factors, and then discuss any changes with your financial consultant. Taking this step will allow you to keep your life in perspective and feel confident that your big expenses like education and retirement, and your big risk factors like children, parents, and dependents, are under control and on track. Having such good perspective—and finding a trusted advisor who takes your risks seriously and will calmly walk you through the repercussions of any decisions you make—will also protect you from capitulating to emotion when Real Life takes you by surprise. It will be helpful, too, if you fill out the Financial Opportunity Profile Checklist before your visit.

Financial Opportunity Profile Room

This section is to guide you in identifing an asset allocation mix that will help you attain your financial goals. By analyzing your investment objectives, time horizons and risk tolerance, we can determine your proposed asset allocation mix.

Please read and answer all questions carefully.

1. When do you expect to begin withdrawing money from your investment account?

   O Now

   O 1 to 2 years

   O 3 to 4 years

   O 5 to 7 years

   O 8 to 10 years

   O 11 or more years

2. Once you begin withdrawing money from your investment account, how long do you expect the withdrawals to last?

   O I plan to take a lump sum distribution

   O 1 to 4 years

   O 5 to 7 years

   O 8 to 10 years

   O 11 or more years

3. Inflation (the rise of prices over time) can erode your investment return. Long-term investors should be aware that, if portfolio returns are less than the inflation rate, their ability to purchase goods and services in the future might actually decline. However, portfolios with long-term returns that significantly exceed inflation are associated with a higher degree of risk. Which of the following portfolios is most consistent with your investment philosophy?

   O **Portfolio 1** will most likely exceed long-term inflation by a significant margin and has a high degree of risk.

   O **Portfolio 2** will most likely exceed long-term inflation by a moderate margin and has a high to moderate degree of risk.

   O **Portfolio 3** will most likely exceed long-term inflation by a small margin and has a moderate degree of risk.

   O **Portfolio 4** will most likely match long-term inflation and has a low degree of risk.

4. Portfolios with the highest average returns also tend to have the highest chance of short-term losses.The table below provides the average dollar return of four hypothetical investments of $100,000 and the possibility of losing money (ending value of less than $100,000) over a one-year holding period. Please select the portfolio with which you are most comfortable.

Probabilities After 1 Year

	Possible average value at the end of one year	Chance of losing money at the end of one year
Portfolio A	$106,000	16%
Portfolio B	$107,000	21%
Portfolio C	$108,000	25%
Portfolio D	$109,000	29%

5. Investing involves a trade-off between risk and return. Historically, investors who have received high long-term average returns have experienced greater fluctuations in the value of their portfolio and more frequent short-term losses than investors in more conservative investments have. Considering the above, which statement best describes your investment goals?

   O Protect the value of my account. In order to minimize the chance for loss, I am willing to accept the lower long-term returns provided by conservative investments.

   O Keep risk to a minimum while trying to achieve slightly higher returns than the returns provided by investments that are more conservative.

   O Balance moderate levels of risk with moderate levels of returns.

   O Maximize long-term investment returns. I am willing to accept large and sometimes dramatic fluctuations in the value of my investments.

6. Historically, markets have experienced recoveries. Suppose you owned a well diversified portfolio that fell by 20% over a short period, consistent with the overall market. Assuming you still have 10 years until you begin withdrawals, how would you react?

   O I would not change my portfolio.

   O I would wait at least one year before changing to options that are more conservative.

   O I would wait at least three months before changing to options that are more conservative.

   O I would immediately change to options that are more conservative.

7. I am comfortable with investments that may frequently experience large declines in value if there is a potential for higher returns.

   O Agree

   O Disagree

   O Strongly disagree

8. Would you like to invest a portion of your portfolio in international investments?

   O Yes

   O No

9. Would you like the ability to invest a portion of your portfolio in real estate?

   O Yes

   O No

10. Would you prefer your fixed income investments to be in municipal bond investments rather than taxable government or corporate bond investments?

   O Yes

   O No

11. Would you like the ability to invest a portion of your portfolio in high yield fixed income?

○ Yes

○ No

12. Would you like the ability to invest a portion of your portfolio in emerging market investments?

○ Yes

○ No

The Financial Opportunities Profile Room demands that you think through the risk factors in your life so you can move forward knowing that you've taken all of them into account. Doing so will thereby free you from numerous anxieties that could otherwise threaten your financial confidence.

MAKE-READY

1. How does your philosophy about money influence your risk tolerance? What adjustments do you need to make?

2. Have you accurately calculated your risk? Do you need professional help to make that evaluation?

3. How are you proactively managing your portfolio?

4. Are you confident that your assets will last you to age 100—or even beyond? If not, what are you going to do about it?

5. Do you know the average rate of return you need in order to achieve your dream and goals?

Chapter Seven

THE CHILDREN'S/HEIRS' ROOM

Remember when we discussed that for a legacy to take hold, it was important to be able to include the people entrusted with its creation? Well, if you look at the Your Financial House template, you'll see that the room below this one is the Legacy Room. Many times the people we identify as the caretakers of our legacy are also our heirs. Often, they are our children or other people to whom we are emotionally attached. And as everybody with a little life experience under their belt can attest, it's the people whom we care about the most, or whom we trust the most, who are also most likely to affect our lives—and our finances, sometimes for better, and unfortunately, sometimes for worse.

Of course, our legacy can be at risk with any heir if we don't plan properly, even when the relationship is not emotionally fraught. Your heirs may include a partner, an employee, a neighbor, or a friend. You may be serving as a mentor to someone who considers you a surrogate parent. One time, for instance, I was helping draft a financial blueprint for a widow. When we got to this second-story room, she explained that she didn't have heirs—no children, no nieces or nephews, not even a godchild. Her family consisted of three dogs and four cats.

Part of my job is to consider all contingencies, so I asked, "How do you plan to provide for those pets if anything should happen to you?"

She replied: "Oh, my neighbors are very nice. They've promised to take care of them for me."

That raised another question in my mind.

"Three dogs and four cats…that's a lot of animals. Have you shared with your neighbor the cost of your vet bills and pet food?"

The woman's expression became worried as she realized that she hadn't considered the financial burden of her pets' care, and she couldn't be sure about her neighbors' ability to bear those costs. Not to worry, I assured her. I then suggested she meet with her estate attorney who suggested she set up a pet trust to secure appropriate funds for her dogs and cats. And just like that, we had furnished her Children's/Heirs' Room.

The point is, no matter who your heirs are, you need to build on the conversations you started in the Legacy Room, and take into account the risks you identified in the Financial Opportunity Profile Room, so you can plan for the needs of those most important to you, prepare them to carry your legacy forward, and mitigate your financial vulnerability while doing it. The Children's/Heirs' Room is where that happens.

Children/Heirs Room

your financial house
the blueprint for financial growth & security

DEPENDENTS

Name	Relationship	Date of Birth	Social Security #	Location	Gender

HEIRS/NON-DEPENDENTS

Name	Relationship	Date of Birth	Social Security #	Location	Gender

Notes: _____

_____
_____

REVIEW ALL OF YOUR POSSIBILITIES

The Financial Opportunity Profile Room gave you a place to assess your risks; this room gives you a place to do some creative thinking about how you might mitigate those risks. For example, it is our job to educate and prepare our heirs so they are ready to handle the responsibilities we ask them to take on, whether it's acting as the executor of our will or managing a charitable donation in our name. If you don't have any direct descendants, that goes double.

One gentleman I knew had been married twice but had no children. He decided he wanted his estate to go to his church. He called his priest, his estate attorney, and me, and the four of us coordinated a game plan for the rest of his life. As his health deteriorated, each of us knew the role we were supposed to play and what he wanted us to do. He lived his final years comfortably in an assisted living facility and was alive when the plans were finalized to build a gym in his name at the church.

Many people who do have direct descendants will realize in the FOP Room that as they save for their children's college educations and their own retirement, there's a good chance they will also be responsible for the cost of their parents' care. That's the kind of thing you want to try to think about ahead of time, because it's easy to get caught up in the emotion of the moment and make unnecessary—even imprudent—sacrifices when it comes time to finance a loved one's needs. Even when aging adults are financially independent, many will eventually need help with the daily tasks of life. If dementia is a factor, those decisions can be more difficult.

Try to consider the consequences of multiple scenarios. Your spouse could retire early to care for your father-in-law, but how would that early retirement impact your financial house? What would be the outcome if you explored the cost of professional geriatric service providers? Make sure you thoroughly research the kinds of benefits to which your father-in-law might be entitled. I remember a man whose children weren't yet out of college and whose father was ninety years old and reaching the stage where he could no longer live alone in his own home. The son was considering altering his home so that his father could move in with him and his family. The resulting $20,000 remodel would make the home accessible to his father, but it was unlikely to positively affect his property value. There was also no guarantee that his father could remain in the home for any length of time.

Meanwhile, the elderly father was reluctant to move in with his son. He was more interested in moving into some sort of assisted living facility. Yet the son knew that assisted living was too expensive for his father's monthly budget to cover.

That's when they came to me. I asked if the father was a veteran. The gentleman had indeed served his country and was entitled to benefits he had never claimed. Our staff then walked father and son through a process that allowed the father to access both appropriate care and his desired level of independence. That solution allowed the son to keep his financial reserves and real estate values intact, while the father was allowed to live with the dignity he deserved.

I've seen it all: a father with a son dying of AIDS; a woman with a drug-addicted daughter; a man who wanted to support his recently divorced, stay-at-home daughter and her three children. I found out about each of these situations when the parents called to tell me to get more aggressive with their investments because they needed to adapt to an unanticipated situation. Rather than put their nest eggs at risk, though, I walked them through the A.S.K. process to find other financial strategies that would offer some help to their children without ruining their chances of reaching their own goals.

START EARLY

One benefit of having your children also be your heirs is that you have a chance to influence them from a young age. If your heirs are your siblings or the people that run your favorite charitable organization, there's not much you can do now to shape them. They are who they are. But with kids you have a chance to shape their approach to life and teach them to share your values so that by the time they're ready to inherit your legacy, financial or otherwise, they know how to preserve it, seek to make it grow, and use it for the benefit of others. Of course, even the best parents have seen their children make choices that disappointed them and even threatened everything they've worked to build. But when you have a family, wealth creation is not just about getting a specific return on your investments; it's also about creating a type of whole-family wealth which makes it less likely—that is, mitigates the risk—that your adult child will move back in with you, or that you'll be paying their rent after they're married.

For example, most parents start to fret over college costs from the minute they find out they're pregnant. No surprise, then, that when most financial advisors meet with clients who have kids, they focus their conversation on how much the family needs to save for college. But focusing exclusively on college savings is too shortsighted. How far a family's college savings will go depends entirely on what kind of person the college student is. If he's motivated and studious, and will use his time at university to build the skills that will make him not only a thoughtful citizen of the world, but an employable one, too, then the family won't need to save quite as much as the family whose college student lacks direction or ambition, and takes his partying more seriously than his studies. That student could take a heck of a lot longer to get through school, so the family's money will have to stretch farther.

And how do you increase your chances of getting the first kind of kid rather than the other? It starts when our sons and daughters are young, when you have a chance to instill in them a love of learning and a desire for excellence. You can't hope your children will earn academic scholarships if you haven't helped them become the kind of student that earns academic scholarships. Of course, there are other kinds of scholarships, many which are offered to students already enrolled in college; but again, their availability will depend entirely upon the decisions your child makes and the attitude she takes toward her education. You can spend a fortune on private education, but that won't necessarily help your child if she doesn't have ambition or a thirst for knowledge.

In addition, many students enter college or even graduate with advanced degrees, yet have no idea how to use their talents, abilities, and strengths to fulfill their potential. Even after working diligently at their studies and spending someone's hard-earned money on tuition, room, and board, some graduates don't know how to apply their degrees to the job market. They may not know how to communicate what they have to offer because no one has helped them market themselves. When an interviewer asks them to talk about what they want to do with their lives, they really have no reply because they haven't been pressed to define their dreams and goals.

Planning for college demands far more than simply putting money aside. It's about figuring out how best to help a child succeed. In the Children's/Heirs' Room you will evaluate each child's strengths and help them improve their weaknesses. It's where you might consider alternatives such as home schooling, private schooling, tutors, or specialized camps, each of which can come with a hefty price tag.

Let me emphasize that when I refer to strengths and weaknesses in children, I believe that this is a huge opportunity to encourage a child to see what he or she is capable of doing in life. I also would recommend having children take a personal assessment that lets them know what areas they are strong in—both in their thinking and in their performance. Kolbe is a company I have used for years with clients, their family members, and with my own team members.

As for weaknesses, it could be that no one has ever exposed the child to an area of learning or sports that allows him or her to excel. In other words, the lightbulb hasn't lit up because the child didn't know better. What may be labeled as a weakness could actually be a lack of exposure. That, too, is one of the values presented in the Children's/Heirs' Room. Seeing a child evolve through high school and college can be an exciting time for a family or parent.

Planning for college also shouldn't be on parents' shoulders alone. In this room you should think about what steps you can take to encourage your child to take ownership of his education. Not only should you explore scholarships and loan options; you should likewise discuss how technology might change the face of education, the rise of online programs, and the possibility of using community college to knock general education requirements out of the way, thus lessening the number of years needed to get a bachelor's degree. You'll want to map out strategies to help your child understand the importance of certain exams, to assist them in identifying their strengths and passions, and to figure out creative ways to introduce them to possible careers that could take advantage of both.

And you'll want to think bigger than college. Think about how to teach your children to make their own decisions so they don't have to move back in with you one day or ask you for help with their mortgage. So many times parents are so focused on reaching a magic college savings number that they neglect helping their students recognize what they really want out of life and what's important to them. Parents need to guide children into considering the kind of person they want to be.

Powell's Law #7: We're all capable of losing millions; very few are capable of making millions. Knowledge and attitude make the difference.

START WHEN YOU CAN

Maybe by the time you start the Your Financial House process your children are already half-grown. That's okay. It's never too late to start having these important conversations. In addition, if you do have older kids, now would be the perfect time to use this room to spend time helping them develop door-opening relationships with advisors and professionals in whatever area of interest your child may have. Those relationships don't happen overnight. Start thinking about your contacts and figuring out which ones you'd be willing to approach on behalf of your children once they indicate through their words, behaviors, and attitudes that they are responsible, mature, and motivated enough to warrant an introduction. The more relationships your children have with such experts, the more doors are likely to open. They will learn how to communicate with adults and how to ask, "How can *I* help *you*?" so they can start building their own legacy.

This room not only helps parents provide for their children, it also helps them teach their heirs to take control of their lives. A lemonade stand at age six might culminate in a tech start-up at age twenty-six. Children need to be taught to market themselves and explore their personal and professional strengths. The more intentionally parents encourage their children's career-skill development, the less likely it is that those youngsters will grow up to become adults who must fall back on Mom and Dad later on. Helping a child develop this sort of confidence creates whole-family wealth. If you apply these preparation principles while saving for college, your child will be more likely to internalize values that enable him or her to be independent, determined, and confident. That child can move forward to reach his or her own dreams and goals, allowing the proud parents to cross one of theirs off their lifetime to-do list.

TEACH THE BIG PICTURE

There's a bigger lesson to be developed in the Children's/Heirs' Room beyond ensuring that children get the education they need to pursue a career path they enjoy and which allows them to make enough money to support themselves. Families should use this space to decide how they will teach their children to build wealth and use money as a tool for good.

Ideally, you want to initiate an ongoing dialogue about money when children are young. Just as you did on your own in the Room of Dreams, you can ask children of any age about their current goals and future dreams. Explain that you'd love to help them reach some of those dreams and goals if they are willing to do their part and put in the effort. Talk to them about saving, spending, and putting money aside for charity. They can begin with you as their "banker," learning to save for short- and long-term goals. They can learn how to budget their school lunch money and their spending money. Discuss the family finances—mortgage costs, grocery expenses, and the cost of private school—to the extent you're comfortable with, but enough so they gain an understanding of what life can cost. Let them in on what sacrifices your family makes to be able to afford things you believe are important.

And as they get older, help your tweens and teens understand that while discretion is a valuable trait, money cannot be a taboo subject within an open, honest relationship. As with attitudes toward children and sex, a couple's fundamental attitudes toward money will profoundly affect their relationships. That doesn't mean they should avoid relationships with people who have less money than they do; you don't want to raise snobs and gold diggers. It just means trying to instill a sense of financial practicality before your children meet the person who lights the stars in their eyes.

I've seen firsthand what can happen when these lessons aren't taught soon enough. A client's daughter fell madly in love with a young man while she was in college. On the cusp of graduation, the couple became engaged. By the time the parents came into my office for the annual update of their financial blueprint, the daughter's wedding plans were going full steam. As the parents explained those plans, I suggested they have a chat with their daughter to ascertain whether she knew about her fiancé's finances, which were, of course, about to become her own. I framed it as an important planning aspect for her marriage. The parents were so engrossed in the excitement of the wedding, however, they never got around to that discussion.

It wasn't until 120 days into the marriage that the young lady learned that this super guy she married had accrued more than $100,000 in student loan debt. The parents had spent lavishly on the wedding. Now they were worried. How would the young couple pay that debt with their modest salaries? Should they help the kids out by paying off the loan?

Once again they came to my office, this time to discuss how they might be able to reconfigure their financial blueprint to help the young couple. It was a shame. They had been so close to getting to the goals they had set up years earlier, and now they were considering sacrificing it all. In addition, I worried that a bailout could have long-term ramifications on their relationship with their daughter and her husband. I would never have suggested their daughter not marry a man she loved because of his debt; but perhaps if her parents had engaged her in regular, frank discussions about money earlier, the girl could have planned ahead, worked with her fiancé to solve the problem, and started a life together relying on each other instead of Mom and Dad.

It's not always easy to talk about money with children, but it's unfair not to. It's natural for parents to want to give their children money, but if you want your kids to be self-sufficient, independent, and prepared for life, you've first got to give them the right tools, and financial literacy is one of them. This is especially important when there's a special needs child in the family. It's shocking how many parents I meet who assume that siblings will take care of their special needs child once they are gone. It can create quite a burden for those siblings. What if they marry someone who is either unwilling or unable to assume that responsibility? What if they aren't quite as financially successful as the family predicts? What if they wind up with their own health concerns? In these circumstances, parents need to prepare their children well ahead of time for their future responsibilities, not by laying the burden on their shoulders but by involving them in the planning process and, even more important, showing them what a privilege it is to live in a family that knows how to pull together and take care of each other.

Ultimately, your goal in this room is to help your heirs build their own financial house. The caretakers of your legacy will do a better job of carrying it forward and building upon it if you share with them what you've learned while building yours.

MAKE-READY

1. If you were in an accident today, who would your heirs be? How have you prepared ahead for those who are dependent upon you?

2. Are you honest with yourself about potential Real Life challenges? What clouds might be on your financial horizon? What issues might you need to anticipate and discuss with a professional?

3. Are you mentoring, educating, and/or communicating your values to the people whom you have chosen to be your heirs? How are you helping them define and realize their dreams and goals?

4. Are you teaching others how to use money responsibly? What adjustments do you need to make in your approach?

5. Are you confident that your heirs will draft a financial blueprint that will ensure that their inheritance is not squandered? Would you be able to help them draft one? Would they allow you to?

6. Have you made it clear to your child that you will help him or her only so much and with a limited amount of financial resources?

Chapter Eight

THE RETIREMENT FULFILLMENT ROOM

You were prompted to identify your retirement goals a long time ago, in the Room of Dreams. Then you calculated how much money you would need to reach them during your time in the Financial Opportunity Profile Room. In fact, you could say that most of the information in this book prepares you in some way or another for your life as a retiree. So why do we now need a whole separate room dedicated to retirement? We don't. We do, however, need a room dedicated to making sure you actually enjoy it. That's why this is called the Retirement Fulfillment Room. You know what you need to survive financially in retirement, but you want to make sure you thrive there, too.

For some, after spending so many years working, the reality of what a bank account looks like without a monthly paycheck can be a bit of a shock. These people usually spend their first few years of retirement blissfully checking off the items on their bucket list. (As you learned in the Financial Opportunity Profile Room, it's during the first three to five years of retirement, in fact, that people usually spend the most money.) Then the novelty wears off, the bucket list is complete, and they find themselves looking at their bank statements realizing that there's no money coming in to replace the sums they just spent. And just like that, they go from an attitude of abundance to an attitude of scarcity. They suddenly feel hemmed in and worried. That's no way to live. To avoid finding yourself in that position, you want to look for activities that will keep you fulfilled and to create a blueprint that will grow your money at a rate that can at least partially replace anything you spend.

Others discover that fulfillment doesn't look the way they thought it would, and that they have to start thinking about a whole new set of issues. Like lunch. Let me explain. It may seem impossible to imagine that a safe, secure retirement could be anything but bliss. Finally, you'll have all the time in the world to do those things you always said you'd do, and to visit those places you said you'd visit. No more alarm clocks, no more business clothes, no more workplace stress and pressure. To most it's heaven. But believe it or not, to some it's hell.

I find that it's mostly men who find themselves in this dilemma. In general, women seem to love retirement (unless they are entrepreneurs, who are usually a special breed that never really wants to slow down, regardless of gender). They usually have a long list of activities they've wanted to get to; they're involved with their family and charities; they pursue hobbies and volunteer. They've often done a great job of cultivating friends and are good about carving out time to see them in person. It's been my experience that the activities they enjoy are usually not all that expensive; they can pursue them in full without draining their resources.

I believe for most men, it's totally different. Perhaps it will be different for tomorrow's male retirees, but today's often have expensive hobbies and tend to spend money in large chunks on anything from a yacht or new set of golf clubs to fishing tackle and season tickets to sports events. On any given weekday the typical male retiree will have a cup of coffee with his friends. Then maybe he'll play golf. Or maybe he'll hunt all morning, or meet with his woodworking group to decide which table saw he should buy.

Then he goes home around noon and says: "Honey, I'm here. What do you want to do for lunch?" And the wife looks at that husband standing in her kitchen, and she's thinking about all of the things she's planned for the afternoon, plans that don't necessarily include her husband. She definitely wasn't planning to prepare lunch. But there he stands, expectantly.

I've had a lot of wives tell me, "We married for better or worse, not to have lunch together every day."

That's why the Retirement Fulfillment Room is not just about saving and investing. Regardless of whether you're a man or a woman, whether you have plenty of time before retirement or just a few short years, this room will help you finish the story of your life, a story that includes a plan to keep you fulfilled past lunchtime. It will also help you recognize when the time is right to retire, as well as prompt you to think through logistics that often get overlooked as the possibility for retirement approaches. For example, many couples set their sights on retiring to warm climates, or near their children and grandchildren in another state, without stopping to consider that the cost of living and real estate is significantly higher than where they currently live. They move, only to discover they can't afford the relaxing, indulgent lifestyle they had anticipated. On top of that, many retirement communities in the south empty out during the summer as their residents chase balmier temperatures, leaving the new retirees stranded for company and entertainment. There is something to be said for learning to adapt and enjoy life even when it doesn't turn out quite the way we thought it would, but if you ask the right questions now, in this room, you're more likely to avoid unpleasant surprises.

BOREDOM SABOTAGES RETIREMENT

The real problem with retirement is that a lot of people get bored, like the client of mine we met back in the Financial Opportunity Profile Room who lost his savings and his marriage by making a foolish investment in a golf course that never opened. When he and I developed a Your Financial House blueprint, he thought he'd be satisfied with long, leisurely days playing golf, but he was mistaken.

There's nothing wrong with recognizing you've made a mistake. Indeed, that's the beauty of a customized YFH—you can always go back in and make adjustments. But instead of revisiting his financial blueprint and rethinking some of the decisions he made in each room of his house, this gentleman insisted (despite my warnings) on dismantling his Financial Opportunity Profile Room to fund his crazy idea. That one decision ultimately wrecked his entire financial house. He was so desperate to feel important and powerful again he let his excitement get the better of him.

He's not alone. I met a former senior executive whom I hadn't seen for a long time and asked him how he was enjoying his retirement. He told me that life was good; then, unexpectedly, he teared up and said, "I love the time with my wife and grandkids…but all I do is change diapers." This was not how he thought retirement would be.

Some of the worst-case scenarios are the people who decide they will stave off boredom through retirement by managing their own assets. I counseled one executive who worked hard for years, eventually amassing $3 million from stock in the publicly traded company where he worked.

Upon retirement, he told me he wouldn't need my services anymore; he was going to manage his money himself. Tragically, that same man was back in my office less than three years later, his net worth down to $500,000. He hadn't told his wife about his losses in the hope that I could help him repair his $2.5 million problem. Of course, at that point, getting him back to $3 million was going to take a Herculean effort. I told him as much, as well as that I couldn't help him attempt to regain his investment values until he informed his wife about the problem. I never heard from him again.

Contrast these unfortunate individuals with a man I met whose wife was smart enough to insist that he could retire only if he agreed to leave the house every day. He did her one better; he started using social media to invite people to join him for dinner at restaurants around the city. Within months, it had evolved into a full-blown dinner club that meets every week and is sought out by any restaurant that wants to pack its dining room and show off its menu.

RETHINK RETIREMENT

I'm starting to think that retirement might be an outdated concept. This isn't a new idea. It's been debated in the media quite frequently, though usually through a pessimistic lens. It's a well-known fact that most Americans (those who didn't draft financial blueprints, anyway) just aren't saving enough for retirement and will probably have to work many years past the traditional retirement age to afford their lifestyle. But there is a rosier possibility. While some people are indeed working longer because they *have* to, I find that many professionals are working longer because they *want* to. If you love what you do, or if there's something you love that you could get paid to do, why wouldn't you do it?

In addition, "Second-Act Careers" are gaining steam. Increasingly, people are realizing that the skills and intellectual capital they developed in their first careers are transferable to new work. Because they planned well for retirement, they don't necessarily need more money, which gives them the freedom to take jobs that might not pay as well, but do offer extremely rich rewards—making these years some of the best of their lives.

That's how one retired corporate exec suffering from dissatisfaction found a second career as an artist. Originally, he came to me because he had decided he wanted to buy and develop a plot of extensive acreage in the middle of nowhere. Alarmed that he was letting his boredom overtake his reason, I shifted the conversation back to his Room of Dreams.

"Did you ever have a dream in your past, or maybe a goal, that you didn't get to live out?"

This man smiled. "Well, I really wanted to be an artist years ago. But, you know, I couldn't make a living at it. I had a family to support. So I worked my way up the corporate ladder instead."

I pointed out that paint and canvas is a lot cheaper than is rural acreage. As we talked about what he liked to paint, he mentioned he enjoyed architectural art. I reminded him the university within a few miles of his home includes a beautiful campus and suggested that many alumni might love the opportunity to buy paintings of the buildings and landscape surrounding their alma mater.

My client followed up on that idea. Today he's not only making money off his hobby, he has a great reputation as a skilled painter of campus landscapes. His wife says she's never seen him enjoy something so much. In essence, he is writing his "retirement fulfillment story."

Similar solutions to boredom come in many forms. I remember another retiree who told me he was tired both of traveling and of not having anything to do after lunch. So I asked him whether he had any passions he had never fulfilled. His answer surprised me.

"Well, you know, years ago before we had kids, I used to buy old cars and fix them up. I just really enjoyed that. Even now, when a car show comes to town, I still go see them. I really love old cars."

We talked a bit longer, and then I pulled eBay up on my computer screen. We looked at some of the old cars on that site, and my client realized that he and a buddy who shared his passion could buy and refurbish such vehicles. Later, as they got into it, they decided that instead of refurbishing cars, they could break them down to sell the parts for more than they had paid for each car. So now he and his friend have a hobby that's generating some income. He didn't need it; he was set for life. But he loves the challenge, and he's enjoying writing his story.

You have to plan against boredom by committing to growing and reinventing yourself. So many times people spend their working lives thinking about "there," as in, "Someday I'm going to get there." And then one day they get "there," and they have the house, the car, the expensive hobbies, and all of the things they hoped they'd have once they made it, only to discover that none of it is as fun or fulfilling as they thought it would be. So before you get "there," think long and hard about what goals you could set and what good you could do—whether through charity work, organizing social events, or learning a new skill—once you're no longer tied to a strict work schedule. You could even go back to school. Why not? This is America, a place where anyone—even a retiree—can dream and set his or her own path.

Powell's Law #8: Always try to surpass the day before.

To jump-start your thinking process about retirement, fill out the Retirement Fulfillment Room worksheet.

Retirement
Fulfillment Room

your financial house
the blueprint for financial growth & security

CLIENT	CO-CLIENT

What would you like to do in the first 60 days of retirement?

_____   _____
_____   _____
_____   _____
_____   _____
_____   _____
_____   _____
_____

What are some things that you dreamed of having or doing?

_____   _____
_____   _____
_____   _____
_____

What are some other hobbies / activities that you enjoy?

_____   _____
_____   _____
_____   _____
_____   _____

TAKE A TEST-DRIVE

Want to know a good way to "test-drive" retirement to see whether you really want to stop working? Or at least to get a better idea of how you would want to spend your time if you no longer had to report to a job? Leverage your seniority at your workplace. For instance, you might ask your company if you could take a sabbatical (some companies even offer them after a certain number of years of service). At the very least, if you've earned several weeks of vacation, try taking them all, and try taking them all at the same time. Sometimes when people get away for more than the week and a half of vacation most Americans usually allow themselves, they get a chance to realize how much they enjoy their job. Even just two or three months off can help someone who has worked for thirty years gain perspective on what it will be like to be home every day, and whether that's as appealing a prospect as he might have once thought. As tempting as it might be to use this time to travel, you should spend this time in your hometown. Many retirees imagine they will spend most of their time traveling, but you can't travel all of the time. You need to know what an ordinary, calm life will feel like.

In the weeks or months away from work, you may be amazed at what you discover. You may find you are refreshed enough to develop new ideas that would benefit your current company. Or you might decide that although you do want to step back, you'd like to continue to work part-time to help fund something you planned in your Room of Dreams. Of course, you might find that you love not working and confirm that you're going to be perfectly satisfied waking up every morning and improvising your days away. Or you might realize that you're not ready to retire at all. Certain jobs and industries require mandatory retirement at a certain age, whether you're ready to retire or not. If you're in one of them, you'll want to start laying the groundwork for your retirement fulfillment strategy at least five years in advance.

JUST THE BEGINNING

The main thing to remember is that "retirement" isn't synonymous with "over." Retirement should be just the beginning of something new and wonderful. And you know, the same goes for layoffs. That's not to say that losing one's job is reason to rejoice, but it happens with increasing frequency, and it happens to everyone—from the newest recruit to the most senior exec. The Digital Age has brought us into a tremendous economic transition period, and certain careers are going to evaporate, just like they did in the early aughts (when online business really started to take off) and a hundred years earlier at the beginning of the twentieth century. (As Will Rogers said, "History doesn't repeat itself, but it sure does rhyme.") It is no longer unusual for employees in their forties to be offered an early-out package. But if you've been visiting the Retirement Fulfillment Room during your annual visit to the YFH blueprint you created, any unexpected career or job interruption needn't be a disaster, because every time you come in, you'll take the opportunity to make sure you're prepared.

For example, whether you're facing retirement, going full steam in your career, or just starting out, during every visit you should ask yourself:

What is the future of my industry?

Am I still happy working in it?

Am I still making a difference in my organization?

What other jobs might suit my skills and interests?

Your answers will probably change over time, which is why this YFH blueprint must be updated annually. In fact, if you answer these questions thoroughly, you may diminish your chances of losing your job unexpectedly, which means you'll have more time to get ready.

I've included a substantial list of recommended reading in this book, but I want to highlight one title in particular that every working individual should read. It's called *Bold: How to Go Big, Create Wealth, and Impact the World*, by Peter H. Diamandis and Steven Kotler. In it Peter explains that each and every groundbreaking, game-changing, disruptive technology grows the same way exponentially, hitting these six milestones from conception to mass-market adoption—Digitalization, Deception, Disruption, Demonetization, Dematerialization, and Democratization. Recognizing these "6 Ds" can give everyone, no matter their industry, a way to predict the potentially massive changes in their field as well as to figure out ahead of time what skills they need to acquire—or even how they can completely reinvent themselves—to ensure their relevance and career longevity.

If you love what you do and simply want to do it less often or under less pressure, your understanding of the *bold* 6 Ds can help shape your life post-retirement too. Use the time beforehand to sharpen your skills, to network, and to build relationships that you could later turn to for consulting gigs if you wanted. Why do I suggest that? Well, according to a 2010 study by Intuit, 40 percent of the workforce will be freelancers or part-time employees by 2020.[4] Or you could join forces with a younger colleague or business owner in your field, standing in as a substitute or extra hand whenever the need arises.

---

4. "Twenty Trends That Will Shape the Next Decade," *Intuit 2020 Report*, October 2010, 21, http://http-download.intuit.com/http.intuit/CMO/intuit/futureofsmallbusiness/intuit_2020_report.pdf.

No matter how old you are, it is wise to think ahead of time about what would happen if you weren't working; what you could do to assure that you can make ends meet; what kind of opportunities it might represent; and what you'd do with your unexpected free time.

In addition, you'll want to spend sufficient time in this room to ensure you're doing everything you can to stay visible to other people in your industry and beyond. In this day and age, two important tasks to complete will be building your brand and making connections. Let's look further into how the Retirement Fulfillment Room holds the keys to doing both.

BUILDING YOUR BRAND

People can build their own brands now through so many ways, but the truth is, it takes a lot of time and perseverance to do it well. Especially if you're not working full-time any longer, this would be the perfect opportunity to finally figure out how to make Twitter work for you or to build your LinkedIn profile or to network at a local conference you were always too busy to attend. This is a country where people can get second, third, and even fourth chances to re-create themselves if they want to. With a solid financial blueprint to guide you, those moments when you're not working, whether by force or by choice, could be some of the most creative and productive moments of your life.

MAKING CONNECTIONS

Too often clients whose jobs ended long before they were ready to retire express desperation, because they assume they can never make the same kind of money they used to make elsewhere. I always disagree. A walk through the A.S.K. process often reveals better opportunities than they imagined. Sometimes it just comes down to making the right connections.

Just as with building your brand, social media makes it easier than ever before to connect with experts, and many of these people are surprisingly willing to share their expertise with strangers. A considerable number of my clients in career transition have connected with someone through LinkedIn, then picked up the phone or e-mailed that person to ask if they could spare twenty minutes to share his or her wisdom about the industry and offer some advice about how to transition into it. The results have been amazing. Many who have tried this approach have had experts take them to lunch. Professionals are generally eager to share their time and knowledge with someone who is genuinely interested in their work, and if they feel a person is a good candidate for the field, they'll often make new introductions.

You'll find plenty of books that offer advice about how to use social media to make connections. The trick to making those connections lead you to something great, however, is rooted in a lesson that's a little more old school. I myself learned it years ago, long before LinkedIn. I was working with an attorney by the name of Alan Zeigler, who assisted me in designing and developing municipal bonds. I shared my frustration with Alan that I wasn't getting to meet enough people to get business for those bonds. Alan had a great insight.

"It's all in the questions, Greg."

When I asked him what he meant, he suggested I read what is now considered a classic networking book, *How to Talk with Practically Anybody about Practically Anything* by Barbara Walters. She explained that, paradoxically, great conversationalists are not people who talk a lot about themselves; rather, they are people who show genuine interest in and listen to others. That book, which I read in one evening, taught and inspired me to write and memorize a series of questions I could ask each city or county representative I met, the most important of which is, "How can I help you?" (Recall that we first encountered this question in the Legacy Room, where we discussed how helping others is really what building a legacy is all about.) It's a question that has opened countless doors for me.

I've since adapted it into a sort of game, which works like this: Whenever you meet someone new, especially at an event or a social gathering, make only three brief statements that focus on you. After that, everything else that comes out of your mouth should be a question. And these have to be questions you're genuinely interested in hearing the answer to. No, "Nice weather today, huh?"

Here's an example of how this type of conversation might sound.

> Hi, my name is Greg Powell. This is the first Rotary International meeting I've been to. I understand this particular club is growing by leaps and bounds.
>
> What's your name?
>
> What brings you here?
>
> How do you know everybody? How did you/your business get connected with this organization?

Note in this example I make only short statements about myself. I would answer any questions someone might have for me, of course, but I would keep each reply brief because my focus would be on learning more about the other person. My questions would not pry, a surefire way to put people off. Instead, they would invite others to talk about themselves, their job, their company, or whatever else they would like to talk about. Eventually, I would follow up with, "How can I help you?"

Although being a great conversationalist is a rare skill, it is vitally important for all of us—not just those in career transition—to cultivate it. Why? Because the more doors you open for others, the more doors will open for you. Asking, "What can I do for you?" and staying connected, engaged, and relevant will be the key to finding fulfillment at any stage in your life, whether you're in your first or your second act.

People have asked me if there's a chance of sounding manipulative or artificial by asking this question. Not if you're being sincere and authentic. I am always motivated to help others and amazed at the opportunities that question has brought my way. I am convinced that the world would be a better place if that question were asked more often. My dear friend Dan Sullivan, President and CEO of Strategic Coach, believes that most people are striving to have the four freedoms: Freedom of time, Freedom of money, Freedom of relationships, and Freedom of purpose. By helping others, they help you, too, in achieving your goals.

The Retirement Fulfillment Room is built to encourage you to answer the questions that will allow you to guide your financial planner so he or she can help you properly plan for the financial freedom you'll need to live well and pursue your passion, whether that means continuing in your current job or doing something entirely different. Visiting this room every year will ensure that you acknowledge and address any shifts in your field or your feelings about your current work or life, and it will allow you to write a story with a happy ending.

MAKE-READY

1. How many of the goals you listed in your Room of Dreams are likely to be realized in the Retirement Fulfillment Room? How do you intend to make sure your life is full and engaging? What are you doing now to make plans toward that end?

2. Are you confident that you are saving and investing appropriately to maintain or expand your current lifestyle during retirement? If not, what steps do you need to take to feel confident?

3. Are you accessing professional advice? Is that advisor helping you plan not only for your retirement but also for any career transitions you might encounter along the way?

4. Are you making the right contacts to help with your transitions? Are you asking the right people the right questions? Are you getting the answers you need to confidently move forward professionally?

5. What other anxieties about retirement are you experiencing that might be resolved with the help of your professional advisors such as your CPA, attorney, financial advisor, and doctor? You need to ask yourself which professionals have the knowledge that can help you the most.

Chapter Nine

THE ESTATE PLANNING ROOM

At last, here we are. This may just be the most important room in Your Financial House. And yet, it's also the room that people most often resist entering or even thinking about. Why are people so squeamish about discussing their estates? Some people, mostly men, tell me that it's just too terrifying to seriously imagine their own mortality. Others, mostly married women, tell me that the whole process seems overwhelming and time-consuming, and besides, they don't know where to begin because their husbands take care of the financial matters.

All of these reasons, while understandable, are terrible. Not only that, they are dangerous. Here's why:

- The majority of today's household financial information is locked in password-protected online accounts—but the passwords live in only one family member's head.
- In one study, 40 percent of widows reported a "negative life-style change" following the death of their spouse.[5]
- The average human lifespan is seventy-eight years.[6]

5. Richard Eisenberg, "Widows Face Years of Undue Financial Hardship," Next Avenue, April 13, 2015, http://www.nextavenue.org/blog/widows-face-years-undue-financial-hardship.
6. "Fast Stats: Life Expectancy," Center for Disease Control and Prevention, last updated February 2015, http://www.cdc.gov/nchs/fastats/life-expectancy.htm.

- 90 percent of all money left in an estate will be left to women.
- On average, most widows survive their husbands by a decade or more.[7]

Too often people don't understand that *one of their most important wealth assets is time.* Taking time to plan and build your financial house in advance can make a huge difference not only in your level of comfort and security later in life but also in that of your loved ones.

The contents of this room are not primarily for married people, nor are they useful only in the event of one's death. Often, an estate plan is used simply to provide a temporary solution if you become ill; it provides a game plan until you get your health back. It protects your loved ones from being forced to hire an attorney to get access to funds they need to care for you or your interests. The contents identified in your Estate Planning Room can also be used to keep track of the professionals and directives you've arranged for dependents, like elderly parents. And naturally, your estate plan will also be referred to if and when you die.

Since no one likes to think about that, let's think about the living. If you are a married man, imagine what your spouse's emotional state would be in the event of your death. It would be cruel to leave her to play detective to figure out what benefits she has coming to her as she struggles through her grief and tries to keep the rest of your family together. If you are a married woman, imagine trying to cope with the loss of your spouse and then finding out you can't access any accounts because you don't have the right passwords—or worse, finding out too late that paperwork wasn't properly filed and certain benefits you were counting on actually *won't be coming to you.* And if you are unmarried but over the age of, say, twenty-five, imagine your family trying to figure out how to access your

7. David Latko, "Financial Tips for Widows," CBSNews.com, 2003, http://www.cbsnews.com/news/financial-tips-for-widows/.

finances and accounts even while dealing with the shock of losing you. You wouldn't want to add to their burden, would you?

Of course not. I could write a whole book using real-life examples of people who were highly successful yet didn't address their critical financial issues in the Estate Planning Room. There is no doubt in my mind that every page would be filled with the phrase "You wouldn't want to…" to which the person always answers, "Of course not." Most of us don't want to cause our loved ones pain. But that's what we risk doing if we don't spend enough time in the Estate Planning Room. All along as I've discussed your financial goals and how to best furnish the rooms in Your Financial House as you seek to achieve them, I've also asked you to consider the relationships that could affect those goals. Now is not the time to make mistakes, because you won't be able to fix them when you're gone, and the consequences will forever follow all of the people affected. Building this house is the equivalent of building your financial confidence. Let's make sure we give that gift to everyone around you as well.

WHAT DO YOU KNOW?

First, you need to know what you know. Second, you need to understand how many people your health can impact. Third, you will realize that a beneficiary form can be just as important as the will. Fourth, you will need to realize that the legal documents in your Estate Planning Room are important to all of the other rooms in the YFH process. So let's start with the first item: you need to know what you know. The best place to find this out is by completing your Estate Planning Room punch list. Take a look at the form below and fill in as many answers as you can.

Estate Planning Room

your financial house

	CLIENT		CO-CLIENT	

	CLIENT			CO-CLIENT		
Do you have current Wills?	Yes	No		Yes	No	
	Date Executed_____			Date Executed:_____		
Do you have current Trusts?	Yes	No		Yes	No	
Do you have a Medical Directive?	Yes	No		Yes	No	
Location of original documents?	_____			_____		
Who *should be* your Executor?	_____			_____		
Who *should be* your Successor Executor?	_____			_____		
Who *should be* the Guardian of your minor children?	_____			_____		
Who do you want controlling the funds for your minor children?	_____			_____		

Who should inherit your estate at your death and at what percentage?

My Spouse	_____ %____		My Spouse	_____ %____	
My Children	_____ %____		My Children	_____ %____	
	_____ %____			_____ %____	
	_____ %____			_____ %____	
	_____ %____			_____ %____	
My Sibling	_____ %____			_____ %____	
	_____ %____			_____ %____	
My Parent	_____ %____			_____ %____	
	_____ %____			_____ %____	
Church	_____ %____			_____ %____	
Charity	_____ %____			_____ %____	
Other	_____ %____			_____ %____	

How did you do? Can you fill in every blank? Is the page mostly empty? Either way, now you know what you do and don't know, which is half the battle. You've also got a great starting point for when you're ready to meet with a financial advisor.

"Armed with this knowledge already, do I really need a financial advisor?" you might ask.

Allow me to recap by way of answering what is a valid question. In every other room of this house we've toured thus far, I've indicated that the revelations you make will help guide not only your financial planning decisions but also your conversations with a financial planner—should you choose to meet with one. There are, after all, some people who are capable of handling or simply prefer to handle their financial planning themselves. Here, though, is where you don't want to DIY. By virtue of experience and education, a financial advisor will be able to present you with more options to suit your circumstances. Let me illustrate.

Most people know that they can assign a beneficiary to a tax-deferred account like an IRA, a 401K, or an insurance policy, but they don't know that they can also designate a beneficiary on taxable accounts such as bank accounts and mutual funds. It thus becomes a transfer-on-death, or TOD, account. The beneficiary/beneficiaries simply have to present the financial institution with a death certificate and proper identification, and the funds in the account are turned over to them, just like that. It's a faster way to expedite funds to your descendants because it bypasses the probate process, which, depending on the size of the estate or the legalities involved, could take a while. A TOD is thus a wonderful way to make sure your survivors aren't left struggling to pay any of your final bills or funeral expenses. You and your spouse can even set up a TOD with joint rights of survivorship, which means that the account would automatically transfer to the surviving spouse, and when he or she dies, immediately to the next beneficiary listed. This is just one example of the many ways someone with deep knowledge and expertise can help you find the best solutions for protecting your wealth and your family.

Not only do I strongly urge you to consult with a financial advisor; I advise you to speak with a CPA and an estate attorney as well. Yes, *all three*. And see to it that they each have the others' contact information, and that they will be willing to kindly and gently walk your heirs or executors through the process of settling your estate. In this way you've ensured that a surviving spouse or child can seek expertise and advice from someone who is sympathetic but not caught in the family's emotional turmoil.

The reality is that not all financial advisors press their clients to open up their financial planning to their estate attorneys, but you should demand it. You want to protect all of your assets and all of your family members. The combined expertise of these professionals can assure you've done that. This is the team that's going to make sure the arrangements you think you're making are really locked into place; that all of the details have been examined; that you're protected from exorbitant taxes; and that something unexpected can't come along and evaporate everything you've worked so hard to build. I've literally gotten calls at 4:00 or 5:00 in the morning from someone calling on behalf of a terminal client who wants to talk with me one more time in his final days or hours to confirm that his estate plan is in place and I have all of the paperwork his loved ones might need. I've created flow charts to show people how the directions they've put down on paper will be interpreted and executed in the real world—which is a great way to catch problematic loopholes, I might add.

It's one thing to make money, but it's another thing entirely to keep it and protect it. What if a conflict arises between two of your directives after you die? Who would know what to do? It happens all of the time. I worked with a couple who were model clients and had built a truly spectacular financial house. Harry and Helen were very much in love. This was a second marriage for both, and each had children from previous marriages. They came to my office to draft a financial blueprint, and along the way we also figured out exactly how they wanted their respective estates to be distributed in the event of either of their deaths. They took that information to their estate attorney, where they drafted their wills and set up various trusts.

The following year Harry and Helen returned to do their YFH "spring cleaning." As we discussed what had happened in their lives during the year since we had last met, they informed me they had bought additional property. They had placed it in joint tenancy with rights of survivorship, which gave them equal rights to the property, with the property automatically passing to the surviving spouse in the event of the other spouse's death.

It was a good thing they were such diligent financial housekeepers and had come in for their annual review, because it allowed me to catch the terrible mistake they had made. You see, the status of that property nullified and overrode the legal work they had done with the estate attorney. Now in the event of Harry's death, *everything*—not just the new property, but all of his assets—would wind up going to his wife and her offspring rather than his children, as both of them had intended. Their estate attorney could have warned them this would happen, but that individual had not thought to discuss their estate plans when they bought the property.

Why would they? After all, they had married for love and neither one of them was trying to take advantage of the other spouse. That, however, is my point. A review with the estate attorney and the financial advisor could have occurred over the phone or through an exchange of emails. This couple was fortunate it was caught.

Helen was appalled. She had worked hard to form good relationships with her stepchildren, and if this arrangement had been in place at the time of Harry's death, it would have caused an irrevocable rift in the family. Fortunately, that very same estate attorney was able to straighten everything out before any harm was done. Helen and Harry are also excellent examples of why I stated earlier that "Do it yourselfers" (DIYs) can create a mess while trying to save on fees. Just imagine what would have happened if this situation had been addressed without a financial blueprint update.

According to one survey, 64 percent of Americans don't have a will, and over half of those adults have children.[8] It is so important that you buck that trend.

We have all heard people express reluctance to make a will because it could invite an early death. This is a fantastic example of where fear and anxieties prevent someone from moving forward to do what is right for them and their loved ones. We all know that we aren't getting out of this world alive. Death is tragic enough, but why have a fatal ending to your life's story because you didn't take care of your financial affairs in the proper way? One of the greatest acts of love you can show is that you cared enough to take care of your loved ones even after you were gone. The opposite of this can leave major bitterness, resentment, confusion, and a tarnished legacy of your life.

In the YFH process, the financial advisor is there to guide you in understanding the importance of having estate work done to protect your assets. It is not the role of the financial advisor to provide the legal advice and paperwork. That responsibility goes to the estate attorney, who creates such legal documents as the will. All too often, however, a client never introduces the financial advisor to the estate attorney, or vice

---

8. "Rocket Lawyer Delivers No Excuses Estate Planning for April 'Make-A-Will Month,'" *Rocket Lawyer News*, https://www.rocketlawyer.com/news/article-Make-a-Will-Month-2014.aspx.

versa. Facilitating communication among these professionals will help you enhance your financial success.

Let me emphasize that you should use an attorney who specializes in estate law. Give her a copy of your financial blueprint so she can fully understand your whole picture. Have her write a will for you and sign it before two witnesses. Don't make people guess what you would want to see happen regarding your money, your children, or your house—they're likely to guess wrong. And if you have children, it's imperative that you write out a will as soon as possible. If something should happen to you, you don't want a single day to go by where there is any uncertainty about where they are supposed to go or who is going to take care of them.

Not only that, if you die without a will, you could set the scene for a terrible battle if family members disagree over what would be best for those children. If you are divorced, it is likely that you would want your children's other parent to take custody of the kids, but would you want them to have unfettered access to the kids' money too? Various arrangements can be drafted to ensure that your ex-spouse is limited to spending your money on your children, not on a new family that may come along in the future. In addition, you'll want to make provisions for what will happen to the children's money should your ex-spouse predecease you.

Too much is at stake for you to keep putting off writing a will. Good intentions count for very little in the Estate Planning Room.

Now, let's say you do have a will, and many of the other documents listed on the punch list. I'm afraid you're not done. Just because you've filled out your Estate Room checklist does not mean you shouldn't come back to this room again and again. In fact, this room will need your attention throughout your lifetime, because life has a funny way of changing as the years go by. What was appropriate when you were younger may no longer be; what makes sense to you now may not in a decade. If you don't keep your Estate Planning Room up to date, it's possible your executors won't be able to handle your estate the way you intended; as a result, your heirs could be shortchanged. Coordinate a team made up of a financial planner, a CPA, and an estate attorney, and regularly review your YFH blueprint with them and with your spouse and family members so that everyone knows what to do when it's your time to go.

SUGGESTIONS FOR A SOLID ESTATE PLAN

As a financial advisor I wouldn't presume to offer legal advice, but I've watched heirs cope with a number of awkward and even tragic financial situations following a client's death that could have been easily avoided if the client had just followed a few of the simple suggestions below. Keep them in mind when you meet with your estate lawyer to plan your estate and discuss the issues surrounding these suggestions before you make and record any final decisions.

DON'T TURN TO JUST ANY LAWYER TO PLAN YOUR ESTATE

Estate attorneys are highly specialized and will be able to protect you from the multitude of pitfalls and complications that can arise in this complex legal process. Clients frequently will ask a friend or family member who happens to be a lawyer to do them a favor and save them some money by handling their estate paperwork. Just about any lawyer can do it, but they'll be working with a template that doesn't take into account your individual needs. Many times, clients who didn't want to invest in an attorney who specializes in estates will discover a big mistake somewhere down the line. Or worse, their heirs will. It's just not worth the risk. Don't ask your cousin the real estate attorney to help you with this. In fact, don't ask any family members to help you plan your estate. You need to work with an estate attorney and a financial advisor who will uphold the confidentiality of your will and your wishes/requests. You need to be able to think clearly in making your estate decisions. In no way do you need the worry that a family member could learn of your estate or money issues prior to your death. People are busy and it's too easy for them to push your needs off to the side while they attend to their paying clients.

DON'T ASSUME YOUR WILL IS YOUR STRONGEST DOCUMENT

It's easy for people to assume that a signed will is ironclad and guarantees that their wishes for the distribution and allocation of their estate will be followed upon their death. What most people don't realize, however, is that the beneficiaries they list on their accounts *trump any instructions in their will.* I know of an instance in which a man died, and though his will stipulated that all of his assets should be divided equally among his biological children and his stepdaughter, his stepdaughter was the only person listed as the beneficiary on certain accounts. Thus, she was the only person entitled to that money. The biological children were certain their father simply meant that the stepdaughter should act as executor of those accounts and distribute them as indicated in the will. She, on the other hand, insisted the father knew what he was doing and meant for her alone to inherit that money. Unfortunately, no one will ever know with 100 percent certainty who was right, but in the eyes of the law, the stepdaughter was legally entitled to those funds. There would have been no question, however, if the patriarch had made sure that both his financial advisor and his estate attorney were communicating with each other about the clarity and uniformity of the language in the documents they each drew up on his behalf.

A DURABLE POWER OF ATTORNEY IS EVEN MORE IMPORTANT THAN A WILL IS

In order for your will to go into effect, you have to die. A durable power of attorney, however, enables you to grant a trusted individual—usually a family member or close friend—the right to make legal, health care, and financial decisions on your behalf in the event you become too incapacitated to make them yourself. Let's say you have a will in place but you suffer a stroke. Without that durable power of attorney, your caretaker would have to get a court order to be recognized as your guardian. On top of that, you could open up avenues for conflict between family members who disagree about the kind of care you should receive. These cases can be a terrible drain on people's time, money, and emotions, yet all of that is eliminated when one handles one's affairs proactively.

It has been said that if you draft your estate plan as though you had to look your heirs and executors in the eye when they receive it, you will be able to leave a lasting legacy of kindness and compassion. This is by no means a guarantee. In fact, the life you live in the eyes of others will define your legacy in the future.

Powell's Law #9: A legacy and estate are created long before you are gone. Live each day as though it were your last.

Sometimes it's the financial planner or attorney who notices that a client is dealing with dementia and therefore mentally incapable of discussing her finances. If a durable power of attorney has been assigned, the financial planner or attorney can contact the person who has the durable power of attorney and ask that person to join in the discussion and process. This is an excellent way to make sure that the client's original intentions are honored.

This is the kind of thing you want to take care of long before you suffer any health concerns. The plans you put into place now will protect you at a time when you would otherwise be vulnerable. Better to have your durable power of attorney in place, as well as all of the other legal documents we discuss in this chapter, as soon as possible. Because, really, you never know.

MAKE SURE YOU FINALIZE ALL OF YOUR LEGAL PAPERWORK

The following conversation actually happened in my office:

> Me: "Do you have a will?"
>
> Husband, nodding: "Yes, we do. We took care of that several years ago."
>
> Me: "I'd love to see your will, and all the other documents that go with it, like the durable power of attorney."
>
> Wife, passing me papers: "Here they are. But they're not signed."
>
> Husband: "What do you mean they're not signed?"
>
> Wife: "Well, honey, the estate attorney sent them to us to review. We read them, but we never signed and sent them back."

Needless to say, I made them promise to finalize the papers that very afternoon. This couple had spent a lot of money to draft this important paperwork, but if I hadn't asked to see it, they never would have had a legal will. With further analysis, of course, we realized they had not signed their durable power of attorney documents. These documents are just as important as the will, especially if one of them had had a stroke and could not think clearly. People don't realize that a will is for when you die, but a durable power of attorney allows a designated person to take care of you and your financial affairs should you not be able to take care of yourself.

The other point I want to make here is that the attorney who did the legal work had been paid for the legal documents, but he never followed up with the couple to make sure that they signed the documents and returned them to him. This illustrates why I have emphasized throughout this book (and why the YFH process makes certain) that communication occurs between your financial advisor and other professionals you retain. As the saying goes, trust but verify. The YFH process does just that for our clients.

ALWAYS DOUBLE-CHECK WHO YOU'VE NAMED AS YOUR BENEFICIARY/ BENEFICIARIES

I've seen a husband unable to collect the auto insurance after his wife's fatal accident because she had forgotten to include him on the policy after they married. I've counseled a wife whose husband never reviewed the beneficiary information on his 401K and IRA, which meant that upon his death all of his assets went to his first wife, with whom he hadn't had contact in years. Some accounts have provisions in place to help avoid these situations, but not all. Play it safe: every year, and any time there's a major change in your life—a new marriage, the birth of a child, a divorce, the death of a parent—review the beneficiaries you have listed on your accounts to ensure that the funds will be left to the people or organizations you intended.

DON'T LIST "ESTATE" AS YOUR BENEFICIARY

People sometimes list "Estate" as their beneficiary because it's easy and doesn't force them to think about their family dynamics, or because an insurance salesperson trying to get the deal done quickly assures them it's a perfectly good option—which clients can always go back and change later. But they usually don't. If you die and you have "Estate" listed as your beneficiary, your heirs or your executor have to go through the courts to settle the details. The process, called probate, can be a long and costly one. In some cases it can take years and thousands of dollars' worth of court and attorney's fees before heirs receive their inheritance or for executors to even get access to the accounts they were counting on to help them do what you asked them to do. It's a hassle and an expense that you can easily prevent.

DON'T FORGET YOUR PETS

It's the rare attorney who will remember to ask you about what should happen to your pets when you die. If you are single, make sure you keep their needs in mind so that they don't wind up on the street or at the pound. And make sure to set some money aside for them if you have a geriatric pet that requires special medications, food, and frequent veterinary visits, or even if you want to plan ahead for your puppy's old age. Those costs can add up fast, and you don't want to burden whoever agrees to take in your animal friends.

Remember when we were in the Children's/Heirs' Room and I told you about a lady who had three dogs and four cats—each of which was special in her life? As we entered the Estate Planning Room in our discussion, we continued to talk about how she wanted her pets to be taken care of if something happened to her. We discussed how she needed to meet with her estate attorney to set up the pet trust to hold the money to take care of her pets. Her eyes were brimming with tears as we talked, and at a pause in our conversation she said: "Thank you for asking about my pets. They are my children. No one—not even my attorney—has ever asked me how I planned on taking care of them." Needless to say, this one YFH question had opened up a door in the Children's/Heirs' Room and the Estate Planning Room—just one of the many ways I could show you how all of the rooms in the YFH process are connected.

SHOW YOUR APPRECIATION TO YOUR EXECUTOR

Don't underestimate how much work it takes to be the executor of someone else's estate. Executors can turn to estate attorneys for some guidance, but they themselves generally have to do a lot of legwork, fact-finding, and paper processing, all while dealing with questions and concerns from other family members. It's a big job. I would recommend arranging that your executor gets paid for this work, perhaps by receiving a percentage of the estate or as the beneficiary of an insurance policy, annuity, or a 401K, even if he or she volunteers to be the executor of your estate free of charge. These funds will help offset a number of costs—including travel expenses—that neither of you probably realizes executors have to front before beneficiary and inheritance money can be released. Likewise, these funds will compensate executors for the time they spend fulfilling their responsibilities, which can include anything from selling a house to tracking down a long-lost nephew who lives off the grid.

ORGANIZE YOUR DOCUMENTS

You will do your executor a huge favor by taking the opportunity now to organize all of your paperwork and file your documents in one easy-to-find place in your home so he or she can locate them quickly if the need arises. If you keep everything in a bank safety deposit box, make sure your executor knows about it and how to access it. Leave a well-laid-out paper trail so that your estate can be settled quickly and efficiently, with as little confusion or drama as possible.

When we organize our clients' paperwork, we categorize it according to the labels "Financial Advisor," "CPA," and "Estate Attorney." That way the executor doesn't have to guess which document needs to be discussed with whom. Also, if they don't suggest it themselves, ask your advisors to keep copies of these documents to open the door for those initial conversations they will have to have with your executor.

Another good idea is to list on an index card—or if you are tech savvy, on a clearly labeled thumb drive—all of the places where you have assets and policies, the names, e-mail addresses, and phone numbers for your contacts there, as well as the contact information for any other professionals you have worked with on your estate plan. It will give your executor an easy reference point so she doesn't have to go digging through stacks of papers every time she needs to make a phone call.

You're not in the habit of wasting money now; there's no reason to waste any once you're gone, either. The more organized you are, the fewer fees your executor will have to pay to get the paperwork in order and your estate settled.

DON'T LET INDECISION STOP YOU FROM TAKING ACTION

I can't tell you how often a couple tells me they haven't done any estate planning because they can't agree on the executor of their will, or whether his mother or her mother should be the guardian of their children. Even if you haven't made these decisions, make an appointment to meet with an estate attorney. As an impartial observer, this specialized attorney will be able to offer some clear-eyed perspective on your best options. An experienced estate attorney will also be able to suggest a variety of solutions to your dilemma you might not have considered. For example, perhaps you could ask one mother to be the executor and the other to be the guardian. Or did you know that a financial institution could serve as trustee? Someone familiar with the process and an understanding of how tricky family dynamics can be will be able to propose an arrangement bolstered with a system of checks and balances that will give you peace of mind.

DON'T ASSUME EVERYONE WILL BEHAVE

Speaking of tricky family dynamics, you'd be amazed at how quickly money can bring out the worst in people. It might be impossible for you to imagine that your family could start fighting among themselves over your estate, but I assure you it happens often enough that no family should presume they are immune. Maybe you have a family member who is carrying debt no one else knows about. Maybe there's a child who harbors secret resentments and feels she deserves the money more than a favored sibling does. Maybe your main caretaker feels she is entitled to a heftier portion of your assets than the rest of the family that only came to visit you every month or so. Jealousy, fear, hatred, anxiety, insecurity, grief—all of these emotions can strongly affect the way people think and behave following a loved one's death. For this reason above all else, I urge you to take my final suggestion to heart…

COMMUNICATE EARLY AND OFTEN

You can avoid a tremendous amount of pain, frustration, and second-guessing if you just talk with your heirs and co-executors, as well as any favorite organizations or charities, about what you want to have happen upon your death, and perhaps more important, why. Such conversations might be awkward. They might even cause some friction between you and your loved ones. But take this step while you are still around and can take the time to answer people's questions and offer reassurance when necessary. Consider this act your final parting gift. Having these conversations now might not ease your family members' grief upon your passing, but they will help keep them from torturing themselves with unanswered questions and doubts. Leave them with nothing but good memories and the assurance that you cared enough to handle as much as you could ahead of time for them.

As you can see, good estate planning takes some thought. Each stage of your life requires a new document to safeguard your constantly shifting earnings, assets, and family members. And then it's not enough to just get a bunch of paperwork signed and forget about it. One of the best gifts you can leave your loved ones is a well-managed estate plan, one that reflects an individual who always took care of his or her loved ones' best interests and left them able to proceed with dignity.

The goal of this chapter was to offer you plenty of information to get you started, but it's also to leave you with a lot of questions. My hope is that you will bring them to your financial advisor, your CPA, and your estate attorney and use them as a guide to drafting an estate plan that honors, protects, and carries on everything you worked to achieve during your lifetime.

MAKE-READY

1. Don't let the topic of an estate plan intimidate you. Write on a pad of paper (or type on your laptop) all of the ways you would like to be remembered by family and friends. What would you like to have them say about you? What assets would you leave with them? Who specifically would those assets go to?

2. Make a list of the people you trust to be the executor of your estate, then prioritize the order you want the executors to be in if someone can't serve in that role for you.

3. If you have young children, who would be their guardian? Make a list of people and prioritize who would take care of your children first.

4. List which family members are excellent savers and which ones are spenders. You may decide to set up trusts for the family members who are spenders, into which funds will go in the event of your death.

5. Is there anyone you would like to surprise with a gift from your estate? It could be someone who touched your life or an organization that was there for you during a rough period in your life. Make a list and enjoy how you could make a difference for them.

6. List all of the accounts in your name that require the name of a beneficiary. Have you checked all of those accounts to make sure the beneficiary is correct?

7. Go online to yourfinancialhouse.com and complete the Punch List information, especially the Estate Planning Room. This is the information an estate attorney will need

to do a thorough job in creating your will and any other legal documents you need.

8. Are you having financial planning/estate planning discussions with your financial advisor as they relate to your assets?

9. Are you currently working with an estate attorney who understands your wishes and desires for your estate and heirs?

10. If you are not working with professionals who can help you get started, how do you plan on finding a financial advisor and estate attorney who will add value to this issue in your life? Jot down your thoughts on the steps you need to take.

Chapter Ten

THE ATTIC

As we enter the Attic of the YFH process, I probably owe you an explanation as to how it came about. Recall that *Better, Richer, Fuller* opened with my description of the day my daughter Lydia and I were coloring with Crayolas. I drew a triangle and a square to form a simple house. From that moment, as the YFH process began to unfold, the rooms were easy to design and label as I applied the principles of financial planning along with the conversations and issues my clients faced in their lives and with their money. But what about the triangle of the house? It was blank. Initially, it symbolized the rooftop of the house, which had to be strong and sturdy to protect the rooms when Mother Nature's fearsome winds and storms hit. That analogy stuck in my head until the day I attended a client's funeral and my analogy turned upside down.

My client Norton was one of the finest men I had ever known. He was always upbeat and inspiring. At the age of ninety-one his heart gave out and he passed away in his big recliner—or as he called it, his "old man's throne." The funeral was a celebration of Norton's life, and afterward, many of us gathered for a meal at the house where Norton and his wife, Ella, had raised two sons and three daughters. I thought I had really known Norton because he had shared so much of his life with me. Yet as his children, their spouses, his grandchildren, and other family and friends told stories, I realized I knew only a small portion of this great man's life. At one point, his son Chad turned to me and said, "Do you want to see the museum?"

"The museum?" I said, obviously puzzled.

"Well, that's what my brother and sisters call it. Follow me."

We walked down a hallway and came to a slender door. Chad opened it to reveal a staircase. As we climbed the stairs, I realized we were entering the attic of the house. "Dad kept everything," Chad said. "It used to drive my mom crazy. She would want to clean this attic out and Dad would stop her by saying it was their history together. That's why he kept it so organized, so that Mom couldn't argue with him. Even she would come up here and reminiscence about the past."

I couldn't believe it. Everywhere I looked there were organized stacks of labeled files and boxes: some contained old photo albums or trophies from when Norton coached the boys in Little League; others held dance recital dresses his daughters wore, yearbooks, memorabilia of family trips—the list goes on. Chad walked me over to one corner of the attic that was lined with boxes labeled "Journals." He said, "This has become a special corner for us. Dad wrote every night in a journal from the time he and Mom married. When she passed away, Dad started writing every night to her like he was telling her about his day or his thoughts at the time. The best parts are when he writes about one of us, whether it was excitement or total frustration. He was always a dad who wanted the best for his family. We've really come to treasure these journals."

I had been speechless all this time and finally said, "Wow, Chad, you guys are so lucky to have this."

"Now you know why I called it the museum. It's our past, present, and possibly future, all in an attic. See that filing cabinet?" He pointed to his left. "We found over $75,000 in savings bonds Dad had saved for his grandkids' college education. The drawer below it had stock certificates he hadn't told us about. There was also a deed to some land that he and Mom had inherited that I think he had forgotten about over the years. Suppose we had just written this attic off as 'days gone by' and thrown it out. We would have missed out on this. We just knew this was a special place to Dad."

Chad and I were eventually joined by other family members and probably stayed up in the attic another two hours looking at items from Norton and Ella's history together.

That night as I was thinking about the day's events, the triangle sitting atop the YFH drawing reminded me all of a sudden of Norton and Ella's attic. How many other clients had I worked with who had forgotten to tell me they had other assets hidden away or located in other places? Had they placed them somewhere for safekeeping and never told anyone else about them—or even forgotten them altogether? I also contemplated how Norton's journals told how he and Ella started out as a young married couple who really didn't have any assets or money, yet Norton had left behind an estate valued at 4 million dollars for his kids and grandkids.

As I reflected on those thoughts some more, I was reminded of Abraham Maslow's theory of human motivation, often represented in the form of a pyramid called a Hierarchy of Needs. At the base are physiological needs that support the higher-level needs for safety/security, love/belonging, and esteem. At the top of the pyramid is self-actualization. Norton's journal paralleled Maslow's hierarchy, describing victories and frustrations as he and Ella advanced through life, career, and family. I then inserted Maslow's hierarchy into the attic of the Your Financial House model. I couldn't wait to ask clients whether or not, even after going through each of the rooms of the YFH process, they still had areas they had forgotten to tell me about. Were there topics from their pasts they had forgotten to share? Did they still feel some of their higher-level needs hadn't been met? Could they sleep at night knowing they had achieved "self-actualization"? I had so many questions I wanted answered to achieve my own goal of making a difference in people's lives and raising the standards of the financial service industry.

Guess what? The results were amazing. Even though we had covered so many questions as we walked through the rooms, when I got to the Attic, I would explain that it represented the past, the present, and possibly the future of a person's life. It also represented a place where they might have placed items to keep them safe or to store them for use another day. Let me walk you through the Attic in the same way I do with my clients.

As I described above, the levels of the Attic are inspired by Maslow's Hierarchy of Needs, which asserts that only as our most basic needs for survival are met can we work successfully on achieving a higher sense of purpose and well-being.

So, let's walk through the different levels of the pyramid of needs, asking a critical question or two at each one to determine our level of satisfaction.

> **Physiological:** Have the decisions you've made in this house ensured that even in the event of the unexpected, your family and you would have reliable and easy access to the quality of life you have grown accustomed to living?
>
> **Safety/Security:** Have your decisions enabled you to provide a physically and emotionally safe environment for your family, and

you? Are you confident that you're secure or, at the very least, on your way to a secure, stable, financially sound future?

Love/Belonging: Do you feel you have enough money saved and working for you that you can survive and even treat yourself and loved ones, enjoy the company of others, and make the most of your life? Are you comfortable with your purchases and lifestyle choices? Do they bring you happiness?

Esteem: Are you proud of what you have accomplished and the safeguards you've arranged for yourself and yours? Do you feel you have earned the respect of those whose opinions matter to you? Are you confident that you have A.S.K.ed enough to know that no matter what life throws at you, you'll be okay?

Self-Actualization: Are you on your way to achieving your full potential in life?

Did any new information or concerns reveal themselves as you mentally walked through the different levels? It could very well be that your answers confirmed that you have covered all of the financial and personal issues in your life. If issues or concerns did arise, that's okay too. The YFH process has a few more topics to address to help you achieve that particular level of need.

One lady who was widowed looked at me and said, "I know I am financially sound, but when you asked about the love/belonging level, I squirmed because I still feel socially awkward without my husband when I'm with our old friends." I told her that because she was financially sound she could afford to find new ways to socialize and "belong." She could join new groups to meet new people. She could host a dinner party and invite the new people she had met. She could travel abroad on a tour conducted by her alma mater. My point to her—and to you—is that the Attic confirms that someone can be standing on a firm basic level in the pyramid yet need additional insight or confidence to move through the other levels of need in his or her life. Completing the YFH process all the way to the Attic—and through the pyramid of needs revealed in that room—should give men and women so much knowledge about themselves and their finances that they will be able to move forward to achieve self-actualization.

Once my clients and I have discussed self-actualization, I suggest that the Attic also symbolizes a reminder for them to jog their memory about any times they have placed an asset somewhere and forgotten to tell someone about it or to document their action in some way for others to find the asset in the event something happened to them.

As I relay these next stories to you, think about any items or investments you have placed in a secure place but haven't told anyone about. Remember, if Norton and Ella's children had not gone through file cabinets in the attic, they never would have found the savings bonds, stock certificates, and deed to a property. The estate attorney working with Norton and Ella didn't even know about these assets, nor did I as Norton's financial advisor.

I once entered the YFH Attic with a client and his wife at the tail end of drafting their financial house blueprint and started casually rattling off the list of items I always double-check. When I asked if they had a safety-deposit box, the wife shook her head and said, "No," but the man's face froze. Not only did he have a safety-deposit box; he had about a million dollars inside it that he never had told anyone about! He had worked hard to save that money because he didn't have a retirement plan. In his mind, if no one knew about it, no one could be tempted to spend it. Yet, if he were to be hit by a bus, for instance, his wife would not have known it was there.

You might be wondering at this point how someone could possibly forget *anything* when every room in the financial house required him to answer so many personal and philosophical questions. I don't actually know how or why, but it happens more than you'd think. I'll say to a client, "Now, is there anything you haven't told us about?" and much of the time there is.

Another example involved a female client who shared with me that when she is going to travel and thus be away from her home for a while, she places her expensive jewelry in tampon boxes she then stores under her bathroom sink. She figured that burglars would never take the time to look there, especially with her alarm system going off. I asked her, "Suppose you had an accident on a trip, who would know to look there? Have you told your daughters what you do with your jewelry?"

"You know, I've never thought about it," she said. "But I would surely come back from the grave if one of my daughters threw those tampon boxes into a garbage can without looking!"

I laughed. "I honestly don't think it would cross someone's mind—even a woman's—to look for jewelry in a tampon box." Needless to say, we made a note in her Attic profile that revealed her secret hiding place for her expensive jewelry.

I've had a client remember $40,000 in savings bonds and $200,000 in stock certificates hidden away in an old desk drawer. This, after having shared with me he owned gold bars, a large sliver collection, a rare coin collection, and much, much more.

It is interesting to note that a person's age and life experiences play a key role in how he or she answers the questions within the Attic. Many of my senior citizen clients—especially those who experienced deprivation during the Great Depression—have hidden their money between the pages of books or other items. There are also those senior citizens who have invested in dividend reinvestment programs with various publicly traded companies who forget to tell their adult children they bought the stock many years ago. We can track down the income tax return, but knowing where the original stock certificate is located or who we can get in touch with to determine how much the person actually owns can be a frustrating journey at times.

It is my sincerest hope that when you finish touring the Attic you will pause and smile. The Attic is where we wrap up everything, where we take a look below us and find we've built one heck of a nice house. I have to emphasize, however, that just because you've completed your tour of the Your Financial House process, it doesn't mean you've finished the construction. At our firm, we require our clients to do an annual update— whether they think they need it or not. I always say that, in reality, for a physical house to keep its value or to appreciate in value, the owner needs to oversee its upkeep, renovating and repairing when necessary and even cleaning a room that hasn't been well taken care of by the owner or those living inside. The same runs true for Your Financial House. Every year the blueprint for your own financial house needs to be reviewed. You are the one who plays a key role in your future and in achieving your goals. Your Financial House gives you the financial blueprint to stay focused and confident about how you can achieve those goals.

Powell's Law #10: The only obstacle you have to triumph over in life is yourself.

MAKE-READY

1. Go through each level of the pyramid of needs that I presented in this chapter and ask yourself the questions once again. Write down your answers. If you don't get to self-actualization, ask yourself what steps you need to take to achieve this level.

2. If you have hidden any assets from others, make sure you at least make your financial advisor or estate attorney aware of them. Worst case, write out a list of your assets, place the list in a sealed envelope, and give it to your estate attorney to be opened in the event of your death or if you become disabled.

3. Spending time in the Attic may also involve the financial house of a parent or grandparent. Keep in mind that *age does matter.* Try to initiate a dialogue to see if this family member has hidden any assets. Encourage the parent or grandparent to share that information with you or someone else he or she trusts. After all, you may need to use such assets to take care of your loved ones as they age.

CONCLUSION

Several years ago I had the opportunity to hear legendary former football coach and ESPN analyst Lou Holtz speak at a business conference in Lanai, Hawaii. In front of a group of about forty people, he talked about the ups and downs of his career and the things that motivated him. He also followed up on a famous list he had created in 1966, back when he was twenty-eight years old, unemployed, and awaiting the arrival of his third child. Holtz was in a low place, and he decided that to break out of his rut he would list all of the things he wanted to do before he died. When he was done, the list was 107 entries long! In our meeting four decades later, he described what he had done to make sure he achieved those goals. (At the time, he had reached 102 of the 107, including meeting the pope and leading Notre Dame to the national championship.)

How did he do it? One of the first things he credited was the simple act of writing the goals down. He also explained that in order to achieve your goals, you had to figure out what talents you would need to achieve them, who might be able to help you, and what problems you'd need to anticipate. And finally, he said you had to have a plan. I was elated, not just because I'd always been a big fan, but because many of the questions Lou Holtz asked himself on his way to achieving his dreams were excellent examples of how creating a plan for your life can make a huge difference in your happiness and success. Our specialists urge our clients to make a plan for their life that coordinates their financial goals with their lifetime goals. If Lou Holtz can achieve a list of 107 life goals, think what you might do with an organized process to build Your Financial House!

Something else Lou Holtz said had an equally profound effect on me. During the Q&A portion of his presentation, a gentleman asked Holtz: "You won a national championship. You've also been fired from a head coaching position. What did you learn from those two extremes?"

Holtz paused, and his usually genial smile thinned to a more serious expression. He pointed sternly to his questioner and replied, "I learned in both cases I was still Lou Holtz."

It's an answer I've shared with many clients when they lamented not having gotten around to building their financial house sooner. If you're young and just starting out, the advice in this book will help you get an edge on life. But most people wait a while, sometimes long after they've entered the workforce, to start seriously thinking about financial planning. In the meantime, they accrue a little debt, or they save less than they wanted to, or they get hit with an unexpected medical expense. And then they get scared, sometimes to the point where they resist even starting a financial plan because they're afraid to see just how deep a hole they're in.

And that's a shame, because more often than not, I've been able to show clients like these that there are strategies that can help them turn things around and build a solid financial house. You can't let yourself get weighed down by your past, especially your financial past, and allow it to dictate your present and make your goals and dreams feel unreachable. They don't have to be. Whether you are riding high, have been laid low, or are just cruising along in the middle, you are still the same person.

Grab on to a vision or a dream, and work toward making it a reality. In the words of another sports legend, Yogi Berra: It ain't over 'til it's over.

Powell's Law #11: Don't allow yourself to be a financial victim or to be dependent on anyone. Take charge. Create your own economy.

But do start now. The sooner you do, the more opportunities you'll have to tweak and make adjustments to your YFH plan as your life unfolds and your needs change.

Creating a financial blueprint is no guarantee to having money down the road, but the person who commits to one, I believe, has a much better chance of achieving financial success and stability than the person who doesn't. Like most things, the first time you go through the Your Financial House process will probably take a little time, but it won't be hard if you've committed to it. And as the years go by and you meet your goals, or at least start nearing them, your excitement and enthusiasm will increase, and revisiting your house will become easier and easier. You will feel in control of your life.

The best part of my job is the moment when I'm able to show people that the life they always wanted is there, and real, and likely attainable. There are many other ways to achieve wealth other than with money, you know. Career, community, and family are all great sources of wealth. Your Financial House brings them all together under one roof and gives you tools designed to protect them. Building your financial house gives you the opportunity to take charge of your life, to say, "This is what I want, and this is how I'm going to get there." You may not hit your goals the first time. But just remember that failure is not failure unless you give up. Keep moving forward, and regardless of what it takes, get the information you need so that you're never painted into a corner, paralyzed with indecision and anxiety.

I've achieved many of my own dreams by building my financial house, and now I have a new dream: to see Your Financial Houses across the country, so many that eventually people could form YFH communities. It could happen, especially if we start teaching our children how to draft their financial blueprints at an early age. Steven Dubner, coauthor of *Freakonomics*, has suggested that the ROI of a four-year high school or college foreign language program is often minimal. If that's true, I'd love to see two of those years dedicated instead to teaching young adults the basics of financial literacy. Knowledge is a powerful thing, and the ROI is indisputable. Your Financial House could be a tremendous educational tool that helps steer our youth toward a financially stable and secure future.

Many people say they no longer believe in the American Dream, but I know it's not dead. And so do the thousands of individuals who have learned to grow, protect, and pass on their wealth with Your Financial House. I wrote *Better, Richer, Fuller* because I believed that the YFH process was changing people's lives. I hope it will change yours for the better too. If it does, please share this book, not just with the younger generation but also with anyone who could benefit. Another point I want to make is that I wrote this as a twenty-first-century book. Consequently, you did not find the typical charts and graphs about the markets in this book. You didn't read about any investment products you should buy up or get out of as soon as possible. Rather, this book highlights, through real-life principles and stories, that smart investing begins with a financial blueprint *for* you and *about* you...a *Better, Richer, Fuller* you. To go deeper into the discussion you need to visit our websites, yourfinancialhouse.com and fiplanpartners.com, to see the depth and range of the Your Financial House process.

If you already have a relationship with a financial advisor who puts your needs first (not someone who is merely a salesperson), call him or her today and make an appointment. You now have the information you need to advocate for yourself. Talk to your present financial advisor—or find someone who will respect the financial blueprint you've just worked so hard to create; it will bring fresh ideas and perspective toward helping you ensure that your financial house is as solid and secure as possible. It's time to start the dialogue that will help you see the future and move toward making your dreams come true.

I tell all of my clients how strongly I believe in their freedom—their economic freedom. I remind them that the Founding Fathers of this great nation wrote on a single piece of paper the framework, the blueprint, of America. To the British government it was an illegal document. To our Founding Fathers it was a document affirming the unalienable rights of life, liberty, and the pursuit of happiness—the blueprint for economic freedom and more. It's time for you to write your own "Financial Declaration of Independence." Make the decision to move forward. Write what you want to achieve by using the Your Financial House process step by step. Set the time frame to achieve your financial goals and to complete the YFH blueprint. Make Your Financial House a reality. Make your life Better, Richer, Fuller.

If you have questions, don't hesitate to contact me via the fi-Plan website (www.fiplanpartners.com). If you already have a relationship with your own financial advisor, one whom you trust and whose goals match yours, call him or her and make an appointment today. You now have the information you need to advocate for yourself. It's time to start the dialogue that will help you see the future and begin to make your dreams come true.

POWELL'S LAWS

Powell's Law #1: Money doesn't give you confidence as quickly as confidence gives you money.

Powell's Law #2: There is no magic formula. Only your attitude, beliefs, and knowledge can move you forward.

Powell's Law #3: No one can enjoy success or fulfillment without touching the lives of others.

Powell's Law #4: It's okay to have a latte.

Powell's Law #5: A health issue can be a wealth issue.

Powell's Law #6: Risk is the determining factor that brings up or breaks down our net worth.

Powell's Law #7: We're all capable of losing millions; very few are capable of making millions. Knowledge and attitude make the difference.

Powell's Law #8: Always try to surpass the day before.

Powell's Law #9: A legacy and estate are created long before you are gone. Live each day as though it were your last.

Powell's Law #10: The only obstacle you have to triumph over in life is yourself.

Powell's Law #11: Don't allow yourself to be a financial victim or to be dependent on anyone. Take charge. Create your own economy.

RECOMMENDED READING

I'm a passionate reader, and a day doesn't go by where I don't pick up a book looking for a bit of inspiration or knowledge that I can pass on to my clients. I have to agree with Charlie "Tremendous" Jones, who famously said, "You will be the same person in five years as you are today except for the people you meet and the books you read." In my experience, who you become in the future will depend on the books you read and the people you meet. While I can't personally introduce you to all of the wonderful people I've met over the years, I can share with you some of the most influential and inspiring books I've read. The ones listed below are some of my favorites.

CHAPTER TWO: THE ROOM OF DREAMS

The Laws of Lifetime Growth: Always Make Your Future Bigger Than Your Past, by Dan Sullivan and Catherine Nomura, Berrett-Koehler, 2007.

Wanting What You Want, by Dan Sullivan.

What I Know For Sure, by Oprah Winfrey, Flatiron Books, 2014.

The Compound Effect: Jumpstart Your Income, Your Life, Your Success, by Darren Hardy, Vanguard Press, 2012.

The Perfect Moment: Capturing Life's Greatest Gifts, by Andy Andrews, Thomas Nelson, 2015.

The Seven Decisions: Understanding the Keys to Personal Success, by Andy Andrews, Thomas Nelson, 2014.

Go Put Your Strengths to Work: 6 Powerful Steps to Achieve Outstanding Performance, by Marcus Buckingham, Free Press, 2007.

The Charge: Activating the 10 Human Drives that Make You Feel Alive by Brendon Burchard, Free Press, 2012.

The Start-Up of You: Adapt to the Future, Invest in Yourself, and Transform Your Career, by Reid Hoffman and Ben Casnocha, Crown Business, 2012.

Your Best Just Got Better: Work Smarter, Think Bigger, Make More, by Jason Womack, Wiley, 2012.

CHAPTER THREE: THE LEGACY ROOM

A Gift to My Children: A Father's Lessons for Life and Investing, by Jim Rogers, Random House, 2009.

The Art of Possibility: Transforming Professional and Personal Life, by Rosamund Stone Zander and Benjamin Zander, Penguin, 2002.

Discovering the Laws of Life, by Sir John Marks Templeton, Templeton Press, 2009.

How FULL Is Your Bucket?: Positive Strategies for Work and Life by Tom Rath and Donald O. Clifton, PhD, Gallup, 2004.

Stumbling on Happiness, by Daniel Gilbert, Knopf, 2006.

How Will You Measure Your Life?, by Clayton Christensen, James Allworth, and Karen Dillon, HarperBusiness, 2012.

The Last Lecture, by Randy Pausch with Jeffrey Zaslow, Hachette Books, 2008.

As a Man Thinketh, by James Allen, Tribeca Books, 2011. (Originally published 1903.)

Tell My Sons: A Father's Last Letters, by Lt. Col. Mark M. Weber, Ballantine, 2013.

CHAPTER FOUR: THE LIFESTYLE ROOM

Why Smart People Make Big Money Mistakes and How to Correct Them: Lessons from the Life-Changing Science of Behavioral Economics, by Gary Belsky and Thomas Gilovich, Simon and Schuster, 2010.

Why People Buy Things They Don't Need: Understanding and Predicting Consumer Behavior, by Pamela Danziger, Kaplan Publishing, 2003.

Smart Couples Finish Rich: 9 Steps to Creating a Rich Future for You and Your Partner, by David Bach, Crown Business, 2001.

Stop Acting Rich…and Start Living Like A Real Millionaire, by Thomas J. Stanley, PhD, Wiley, 2009.

CHAPTER FIVE: THE WEALTH ROOM

Investing for a Lifetime: Managing Wealth for the "New Normal," by Richard C. Marston, Wiley, 2014.

Invent It, Sell It, Bank It!, by Lori Greiner, Ballantine, 2014.

What I Learned Before I Sold to Warren Buffet: An Entrepreneur's Guide to Developing a Highly Successful Company, by Barnett C. Helzberg, Jr., Wiley, 2003.

Zero to One: Notes on Startups, or How to Build the Future by Peter Thiel with Blake Masters, Crown, 2014.

Stocks for the Long Run, by Jeremy Siegel, McGraw-Hill.

Think and Grow Rich, by Napoleon Hill.

Everything I Know about Success I Learned from Napoleon Hill: Essential Lessons for Using the Power of Positive Thinking, by Don M. Green, McGraw-Hill, 2013.

How to Be Rich: The Success Secrets of a Billionaire Businessman, by J. Paul Getty.

As I See It: The Autobiography of J. Paul Getty, by J. Getty, J. Paul Getty Museum, 2003.

The 5 Lessons a Millionaire Taught Me about Life and Wealth, by Richard Paul Evans, Touchstone, 2006.

The Self-Made Billionaire Effect: How Extreme Producers Create Massive Value, by John Sviokla and Mitch Cohen, Portfolio 2014.

Pour Your Heart into It: How Starbucks Built a Company One Cup at a Time, by Howard Schultz and Dori Jones Yang, Hyperion, 1999.

The Rational Optimist: How Prosperity Evolves, by Matt Ridley, Harper, 2010.

How Did You Do It, Truett?: A Recipe for Success, by S. Truett Cathy, Looking Glass Press, 2007.

CHAPTER SIX: THE FINANCIAL OPPORTUNITY PROFILE ROOM

Abundance: The Future Is Better Than You Think, by Peter H. Diamandis and Steven Kotler, Free Press, 2012.

The Demographic Cliff: How to Survive and Prosper During the Great Deflation of 2014-2019, by Harry S. Dent, Jr., Portfolio, 2014.

Big Bang Disruption: Strategy in the Age of Devastating Innovation, by Larry Downes and Paul Nunes, Portfolio, 2014.

The New Digital Age: Reshaping the Future of People, Nations and Business, by Eric Schmidt and Jared Cohen, Knopf, 2013.

The Clash of the Cultures: Investment vs. Speculation, by John C. Bogle, Wiley, 2012.

Don't Count on It!: Reflections on Investment Illusions, Capitalism, "Mutual" Funds, Indexing, Entrepreneurship, Idealism, and Heroes, by John C. Bogle, Wiley, 2010.

The Age of Deleveraging: Investment Strategies for a Decade of Slow Growth and Deflation, by A. Gary Shilling, Wiley, 2012.

The Thank You Economy, by Gary Vaynerchuk, HarperBusiness, 2011.

Makers: The New Industrial Revolution, by Chris Anderson, Crown Business, 2014.

CHAPTER SEVEN: THE CHILDREN'S/HEIRS' ROOM

Where You Go Is Not Who You'll Be: An Antidote to the College Admissions Mania, by Frank Bruni, Grand Central, 2015.

Average Is Over: Powering America Beyond the Age of the Great Stagnation, by Tyler Cowen, Dutton, 2013.

Another Season: A Coach's Story of Raising an Exceptional Son, by Gene Stallings and Sally Cook, Little Brown and Co, 2007.

The Trophy Kids Grow Up: How the Millennial Generation Is Shaking Up the Workplace, by Ron Alsop, Jossey Bass, 2008.

CHAPTER EIGHT: THE RETIREMENT ROOM

Bold: How to Go Big, Create Wealth, and Impact the World, by Peter H. Diamandis and Steven Kotler, Simon and Schuster, 2015.

How to Talk with Practically Anybody about Practically Anything, by Barbara Walters, Doubleday, 1970.

Get What's Yours: The Secrets to Maxing Out Your Social Security, by Laurence J. Kotlikoff, Philip Moeller, and Paul Solman, Simon and Schuster, 2015.

A Short Guide to a Long Life, by David B. Agus, MD, Simon and Schuster, 2014.

Thrive: The Third Metric to Redefining Success and Creating a Life of Well-Being, Wisdom, and Wonder, by Arianna Huffington, Harmony, 2014.

Making a Life, Making a Living: Reclaiming Your Purpose and Passion in Business and in Life, by Mark Albion, Grand Central Publishing, 2000.

CONCLUSION

Wins, Losses, and Lessons, by Lou Holtz, William Morrow, 2006.

Winning Every Day: The Game Plan for Success, by Lou Holtz, HarperBusiness, 1998.

Start with Why: How Great Leaders Inspire Everyone to Take Action, by Simon Sinek, Portfolio, 2009.

The Score Takes Care of Itself: My Philosophy on Leadership, by Coach Bill Walsh with Steve Jamison and Craig Walsh, Portfolio, 2009.

Eleven Rings: The Soul of Success, by Phil Jackson and Hugh Delehanty Penguin, 2013.

The Butterfly Effect: How Your Life Matters, by Andy Andrews, Thomas Nelson, 2010.

The Essential Wooden: A Lifetime of Lessons on Leaders and Leadership, by John Wooden and Steve Jamison, McGraw-Hill, 2007.

Freakonomics, Steven Dubner.

ABOUT THE AUTHOR

No one is successful or fulfilled unless they touch the lives of the people around them." This is the creed by which Greg Powell conducts his business and his life. Greg is President and Chief Executive Officer of Fi Plan Partners, LLC, in Birmingham, Alabama, and has over thirty years of experience in the financial industry.

He is a member of the Investment Management Consultants Association (IMCA) and the National Board of Directors for the National Federation of Independent Business (NFIB) and is former Chairman of the NFIB of Alabama. Greg is a member and former President of the Board of Directors for Aldridge Gardens, a board member for the Business Council of Alabama, and member and former President of the Board for Special Equestrians.

Actively involved with Samford University, he is on the Board of Overseers, a member and former Chairman of the university's Brock School of Business Advisory Board and currently serves on the Samford Athletic Executive Committee.

Greg and his wife, Peggy, live in Hoover, Alabama. They have three daughters: Sara, Audrey, and Lydia. He is fond of noting that his daughters have been some of his best teachers. They have given him profound pieces of wisdom and insight into how to make his services and strategies more useful.

It was while playing with his children that Greg came up with the model for Your Financial House®, a management tool designed to bring all aspects of financial planning under one roof. Your Financial House® is a unique program that supports clients' efforts to create a firm foundation from which to build wealth.

INDEX

A

Achievements, coordinating goals with, 177–178
Action, indecision in stopping, 161–162
Adams, James Truslow, 3
Alert, staying, 105
American Dream, 8. See also Dreams
    believing in the, 180
    bringing to fuition, 7
    coining of, as term, 3
    defining, 3–4
    pursuing, 3
Annual review of financial plan, 125–126, 151, 174
Anxieties
    in addressing liabilities, 83
    on health, 38
    identifying, 33–34
    knowledge as best weapon against, 4–5
    overcoming, 32
    physical pain from, 41
    sources in overcoming, 32
Appraisal, getting a, 81
Appreciation, showing to executors, 160
Ashe, Arthur, 62
A.S.K. (anxiety, strengths, knowledge) process,
    32–33, 38, 44, 46, 58–59, 88
    in achieving needed solutions, 38
    fear in, 44
    as ongoing process, 38, 39–42
    opportunities revealed in, 140–141
    reevaluating diagram in, 39–40
    walking through, 46
Assertive communication, 7
Assessment
    of anxieties, 35
    of assets in calculating net worth, 78–82
    of investments, 100–109
    of post employment opportunities, 79–82

    of relationships, 106–109
    of risk, 109–110
    self, 52
    of strengths, 32, 35–37, 40, 52–53
    of wealth, 21
Assets
    assessing your, in calculating net worth, 78–82
    defining, 47
    documentation of, 79
    hidden, 168–174
    managing, 16–17
    strengths as, 88–89
Attorney. See Estate attorney

B

Bach, David, 67
Bank Safety deposit box, 161
Behavior, assumptions on, 162
Belonging, need for, 171
Beneficiaries
    assigning, 149
    double checking on, 158
    instructions in will for, 155–156
    listing estate as, 159
Berra, Yogi, 179
Big picture, teaching children the, 124–127
Bold: How to Go Big, Create Wealth, and Impact
    the World (Diamandis and Kotler), 139
Boredom, in sabotaging retirement, 132–133
Brainstorming, 108
Brand, building, in retirement, 140, 141
Bucket list, checking items off of, 129–130
Building tool, money as a, 71
Bull market, 11
Business
    as aggressive investment, 104

assessment of, 104
starting your own, 28–29, 90–91
Business plan. See also Financial plan/planning
  developing, 91
  writing and presenting, 88–89, 91*–
Buy-and-hold-and-hold-and-hold strategy,
  101–102

C

Camp Smile-a-Mile, 58
Career, interest in having a second, 37, 53–54,
  134–135
Charitable organization, linking to a, 58
Children. See also Pets
  assessment of risks and, 109, 115–127
  confidence in, 124
  impact of relationships and, 22–23
  influencing your, 120–123
  ingraining financial responsibility into, 55–57
  need for will and, 153
  passing values to, 49
  reviewing possibilities with, 118–124
  sending to college, 89–90, 124
  talking about money with, 126
  teaching to make own decisions, 123, 124–127
Chrysler Corporation, 29
Clients, felicitation of feedback for, 51
Coffey, Kevin, 67
College
  funding of, 69–70, 120
  planning for, 37–38, 120–122
  sending children to, 89–90, 124
Communication. See also Conversations
  assertive, 7
  between financial advisor and estate attorney,
    155–156
  making change in, 11
  need for early and often, 162–163
Confidence, 7
  in children, 124
  money and, 18
Conflict, resolving between directives, 139
Contingency plans, incorporating into financial
  planning, 15–16
Conversations. See also Communication
  in guiding their priorities, 72–73
  having positive, 27–28
  having with your self, 13
  keeping going, 54–57
  using numbers to guide the, 71–72
Counterproductive, guilt as, 66
CPA, 150

Creativity, as strength, 37, 89

D

Deception, 139
Decisions, teaching children to make own, 123
Dematerialization, 139
Democratization, 139
Demonetization, 139
Depression, 27
Diamandis, Peter H., 139
Digital Age, 138
Digitalization, 139
Directives, resolving conflict between, 150–152
Discretion, as valuable trait, 125
Disney, Walt, 28
Disruption, 139
Diversification, 97–98
Do it yourselfers (DIYs), 152
Dot.com bubble, 98
Dreams, 27–46. See also American Dream
  bucket list and, 129–130
  coordinating with lifestyle, 21
  fulfillment of, 46, 48, 53–54, 65, 77
  goals in, 61
  identifying your, 6, 20, 47, 92, 96
  knowledge and, 43
  legacies and, 53, 59, 137
  listing your, 46
  obstacles of, 32
  putting limitations on your, 61
  second career as, 37, 53–54, 134–135
  size of, 42–46
  for starting own business, 28–29, 90–91
  test-driving and, 137–138
Dubner, Steven, 180
Durable power of attorney, importance of, 156–157

E

Early out package, 27
Eisenberg, Richard, 145n
Emotion
  assessing risk in removing, 109–110
  separating from facts, 15
The Epic of America (Adams), 3
Estate, listing, as beneficiary, 159
Estate attorney, 150–156
  communication between financial advisors
    and, 155–156
  introducing financial advisors to, 152–153
  selection of, 154–155
Estate planning, 23, 82, 145–165, 160

checklist for, 153
punch list for, 147–148
suggestions for solid, 154–163
Esteem needs, 171
Executors, 154
showing appreciation to your, 160

F

Facts, separating emotion from, 15
Families. See also Children
becoming attuned to others' needs, 55–56
discussing finances, 125
Fear
financial planning and, 14–16
knowledge as best weapon against, 4–5
as natural emotion, 34
Feedback, elicitation of valuable for clients, 51
Financial advisors, 21, 152. See also Financial planners
communication between estate attorney and, 155–156
consulting, 59, 150
introduction to estate attorney and, 152–153
meeting with, 84
need for, 149
relationship with, 181
Financial decisions
basing on knowledge, 15
impact of relationships on, 22
Financial Declaration of Independence, writing your, 181
Financial documents, organizing, 160–161
Financial opportunities, 22, 95–113, 116, 118, 129, 132–133
checklist for, 110, 111–113
Financial planners
anticipation of helping people get richer, 3
liking and trusting, 4
Financial plan/planning, 8, 67, 95. See also Business plan
being proactive in, 14–16
as beneficial, 50
blueprint for, 10–11, 53–54, 69, 86, 91, 132, 138, 139, 140, 151
drafting a, 4–5, 10–11, 31, 53, 75–76, 86, 91, 132, 138, 139, 140, 151, 179
establishing goals in, 13–14
fear and, 14–16
following through on, 7
as holistic, 6–7, 22
incorporating contingency plans in, 15–16
laying foundation for, 9–25

as living document, 5, 17–18
long-term value of, 75–76
need for financial advice and services in, 84–85
as ongoing process, 38, 39–42
periodic review of, 75–76, 125–126, 151, 174
questions in building a, 12–13
satisfaction with, 132
success of, 82
as tool, 5
uses of, 77
Financial practicality, instilling sense of, in children, 125
Financial responsibility, ingraining into children, 55–57
Financial strategies, coordinating with goals, 6
Financing, choosing your, 76
Finish Rich (Bach), 67
Fiscal responsibility, ingraining in younger generation, 55
Flexibility, in game plan, 44–45
Ford Motor Company, 29
Foundation, laying, for financial plan, 9–25
401K, 79, 101, 149
reviewing information for beneficiaries on, 158
Freakonomics (Dubner), 180
Fulfillment, 167–175
checking items off, in bucket list, 129–130
of dreams, 46, 48, 53–54, 65, 77
early out package and, 27
retirement and, 23–24, 129–144
second career and, 37, 53–54, 134–135
starting your own business and, 28–29, 90–91
Funding of college, 69–70, 120

G

Game plan, flexibility in, 44–45
Goals
coordinating with achievements, 177–178
coordinating with financial strategies, 6
dreaming about your, 61
establishing new and revitalizing old, 13–14
identifying your financial, 6, 31, 129
rate of return in achieving, 95
for wealth, 20
writing down, 177
Guilt as counterproductive, 66

H

Happiness, Money Myth and, 73–74
Health
anxiety on, 38

as strength, 89
as wealth issue, 89–90
Heirs. See Children
Hierarchy of Needs, 169
Holistic approach, 6
Holtz, Lou, 177–178
Home ownership, as symbol, 24
How to Talk with Practically Anybody about Practically Anything (Walters), 141–142

I
Iacocca, Lee, 29
Identification of anxieties, 33–34
Income, generating desired annual, 101–104
Indecision, in stopping action, 161–162
Influence on your children, 120–123
Insurance policies, 149
Investments
    assessing, 100–109
    business as aggressive, 104
    limiting your, 103–104
    managing, 16–17
    risk in, 4, 99
IRAs, 149
    reviewing information for beneficiaries on, 158
Roth, 79, 101

J
Job
    anxiety over losing, 37
    assessment of, 104
Joint tenancy with rights of survivorship, 85–86, 151
Jordan, Michael, 28

K
Knowledge
    attaining, 32–33
    basing financial decisions on, 15
    dreams and, 43
    as powerful, 180
    seeking, 37–39
    sharing your, 57–60, 65
    as weapon against anxiety and fear, 4–5
    of your net worth, 83–87
Kotler, Steven, 139

L
Larko, David, 146n
Latte Factor, 67
Lawyer. See Estate attorney

Layoff, concerns over, 91
Legacies, 47–60, 70, 71, 77, 92, 96, 115, 116, 142
    dreams and, 53
    getting help with, 52–54, 59
    holding conversation on, 54–57
    perceptions and, 50–52
    planning your, 47–60
    sharing, 20, 57–60
Legal paperwork, finalizing, 157–158
Liabilities
    anxiety in addressing, 83
    listing in calculating net worth, 82–83
Life, living wanted, 70–71
Life span, underestimating your, 103
Lifestyle, 21, 60, 61–74, 77, 92, 96
    assessing, 63–64, 65, 67, 71
    coordinating with dreams, 21
    enhancing your, 6
    taking control of, 45–46
    wealth and, 74
Limitations
    putting on dreams, 61
    setting, 30
Lincoln, Abraham, 28
LinkedIn, 140, 141
Love
    need for, 171
    sharing your, 57–60

M
Make-ready, 8
Mandatory, retirement as, 137–138
Maslow, Abraham, theory of human motivation, 169–170
Men, retirement for, 130–131
Money
    as building tool, 71
    confidence and, 18
    getting hung up on, 106
    myth of, 73–74
    spending, in retirement, 129
    talking with children about, 126
    as tool for doing good, 48
Money Myth, happiness and, 73–74
Motivation, Maslow's theory of human, 169–170
Multiple scenarios, consequences of, 118–119

N
Needs
    becoming attuned to others, 55–56
    esteem, 171

love/belonging, 171
physiological, 170
safety/security, 170–171
self-actualization, 171
Networking, 141–143
Net worth, 21
assessing assets in calculating, 78–82
knowledge of, 83–87
listing liabilities in calculating, 82–83
risk and, 97
Note taking, 25
Numbers
in guiding conversation, 71–72
interpreting the, 65–70
talking about as premature, 5

O

Obstacles, triumphing over, 174
Onward (Schultz), 67
Opportunities, balancing work with, 4
Overestimation, of rate of return, 102
Overspending, evidence of, 66

P

Passions, pursuing, 4
Perception, 50–52
Pet projects, pursuing, 4
Pets
planning for, 115–116, 159–160
setting up trust for, 160
Physiological needs, 170
Planning, taking time for, 146
Possibilities, reviewing with children, 118–124
Post-employment opportunities, assessing, 23
Powell, Greg, 40, 193–194
first law of, on money and confidence, 18, 183
second law on attitude, belief, and knowledge, 42, 183
third law on enjoying success and fulfillment, 48, 183
fourth law on being happy, 69, 183
fifth law on health issues, 89, 183
sixth law on risk as determining factor, 97, 183
seventh law on knowledge and attitude in making a difference, 123, 183
eighth law on surpassing the day before, 135, 184
ninth law on creation of legacy and estate, 156, 184
tenth law on obstacles in planning, 174, 184
Priorities, defining, 72–73
Proactive, being, 14–16

Probate, 159
Punch list, 62–65, 75
Pyramid of needs
esteem, 171
love/belonging, 171
physiological, 170
safety/security, 170–171
self-actualization, 171

Q

Questions
asking the big, 6, 29–42
in building financial plan, 12–13

R

Rate of return
in achieving goals, 95
overestimation of, 102
Reality, making dreams into, 53–54
Reality check, need for, 97–109
Relationships
assessment of, 106–109
impact on financial decisions, 22
Results, visualizing, 16
Retirement
beginning your, 138–143
boredom in sabotaging, 132–133
building your brand in, 140, 141
making connections in, 140–143
as mandatory, 137–138
rethinking, 133–135
sending money in, 129
test-driving, 137–138
timing of, 70
Retirement communities, 131
Return on investment (ROI), 49, 180
Review
annual, of business plan, 125–126, 151, 174
of information for beneficiaries on 401K, 158
periodic, of financial plan, 75–76
of possibilities with children, 118–124
Risk
assessment of, 109–110
intolerance of, 99
in investments, 4, 99
looking for, 100–109
net worth and, 97
taking on enough, 98–99
tolerance for, 22
Rogers, Will, 138
Roosevelt, Teddy, 28
Roth IRA, 79, 101

Rowling, J. K., 29
Ruth, Babe, 28

S

Safety-deposit box, 172–173
Schultz, Howard, 67, 105
Second career, interest in having, 37, 53–54, 134–135
Self-actualization, 169, 170, 171, 172
Self-assessment, 52
Self-perception, 50–52
Seniority, leveraging, at your workplace, 137
SEP account, 79
Shirtsleeves to shirtsleeves phenomena, 49
Single-family office (SFO), 16–17
Small Business Administration loan process, 91
Social media, 133, 140, 141
Spending habits, studying your, 71–72
Stamina as strength, 37
Standard of living, 7
Standard & Poor's (S&P's) 500 index, 96, 102–103
Starbucks, 105
Strategic Coach, 143
Strengths
    assessing your, 32, 35–37, 40, 52–53
    as assets, 88–89
    creativity as, 37, 89
    discussing your, 27–28
    health as, 89
    turning weaknesses into, 36
Success, enjoying your, 48
Sullivan, Dan, 143
SurveyMonkey.com, 51

T

Test-driving your retirement, 137–138
Time, taking, to plan, 146
Tolerance for risk, 22
Transfer-on-death (TOD) account, 149
Trends, being aware of, 105
Trust, setting up, for pets, 160
Twitter, 140

U

Unexpected, preparing for the, 7, 87–90

V

Values
    passing to children, 49
    sharing your, 20
Vision, establishing your, 47

W

Walters, Barbara, 141–142
Weaknesses, turning into strengths, 36
Wealth, 21, 74, 75–93, 96
    assessing, 21
    assessment form for, 81
    checklist for, 75, 79, 80
    goals for, 20
    growing your, 90–92
    health as issue in, 89–90
    lifestyle and, 74
    preserving, 90
    protecting and growing your, 6
What ifs, 15
Will
    durable power of attorney and, 156–157
    dying without a, 153
    importance of durable power o attorney and, 156–157
    instructions in, for beneficiaries, 155–156
    need for, 152
    strength of, 155–156
    writing your, 153
Winfrey, Oprah, 28
Women, retirement for, 130
Work
    balancing with opportunities, 4
    leveraging seniority at, 137
Worse-case scenarios, 132–133
Writing down your goals, 177

Z

Zeigler, Alan, 141